AMERICA the BEAUTIFUL
PENNSYLVANIA

By Deborah Kent

Consultants

James J. Wetzler, Ed.D., Social Studies Coordinator, Pennsylvania Department of Education, Bureau of Curriculum Instruction

Wm. Ray Heitzmann, Ph.D., Department of Education, Villanova University

Anne H. Cook, Editor, *Project 1776, a Manual for the Bicentennial*; consultant to Brandywine Conservancy, Chadd's Ford

Robert L. Hillerich, Ph.D., Bowling Green State University, Bowling Green, Ohio

CHILDRENS PRESS®
CHICAGO

Winter in rural Pennsylvania

Project Editor: Joan Downing
Assistant Editor: Shari Joffe
Design Director: Margrit Fiddle
Typesetting: Graphic Connections, Inc.
Engraving: Liberty Photoengraving

FOURTH PRINTING, 1992.
INCLUDES 1990 CENSUS FIGURES.

Childrens Press®, Chicago
4 5 6 7 8 9 10 R 97 96 95 94 93 92

Library of Congress Cataloging-in-Publication Data

Kent, Deborah.
  America the beautiful. Pennsylvania.

  (America the beautiful state books)
  Includes index.
  Summary: Examines the geography, population, history,
education, culture, and recreation of the Keystone
State.
  1. Pennsylvania—Juvenile literature. [1. Penn-
sylvania] I. Title. II. Series.
F149.3.K46 1988   974.8   87-36754
ISBN 0-516-00484-0

Elfreth's Alley,
in Philadelphia,
is the oldest
unchanged street in
the United States.

TABLE OF CONTENTS

Chapter 1
THE KEYSTONE OF THE NATION

THE KEYSTONE OF THE NATION

When a stonemason fashions the arched entrance of a building, he works with painstaking care. Stone by stone the columns rise, gradually curving inward until they almost touch. At last the mason sets a stone at the very top. It is carved with such precision that it fits the spot exactly and bears the weight of all of the stones beneath. This final stone, known as the keystone, holds the entire arch together, and gives it unshakeable strength.

After the American Revolution, the thirteen new American states formed a long arc up the Atlantic coast. Poised at the very center of this area, Pennsylvania received the nickname the "Keystone State."

As the country grew, the name took on greater meaning. Pennsylvania became a hub of commerce and industry. The port of Philadelphia sent produce and manufactured goods throughout the eastern states. The port of Pittsburgh played a crucial role in opening the western frontier to settlement. Pennsylvania's vast reserves of coal and oil heated homes and fueled factories.

Today, Pennsylvania remains a leading center of mining and manufacturing. Its orchestras and fine museums celebrate the arts and its universities and research centers are monuments to higher learning. Though it has undergone immense changes in recent decades, Pennsylvania still holds a vital position in the economic, political, and cultural life of the United States. It continues to earn its nickname, the "Keystone State."

Chapter 2
THE LAND

THE LAND

Still the pine woods scent the noon
Still the cat bird sings his tune
Still autumn sets the maple-forest blazing.
Still the grapevine through the dusk
Flings her soul-compelling musk
Still the fireflies in the corn make night amazing.

They are there, there, with earth immortal,
(Citizens, I give you friendly warning),
The things that truly last
When men and times have passed.
They are all in Pennsylvania this morning.

Most readers know Rudyard Kipling as the author of *The Jungle Book* and other tales of India. Yet he was so impressed by his view of Pennsylvania that he celebrated its natural beauty in this poem. With its tumbling streams, tree-clad mountains, and rolling farmland, Pennsylvania dazzles the traveler today as it thrilled Kipling a century ago.

GEOGRAPHY AND TOPOGRAPHY

On a map, Pennsylvania looks like a slightly misshapen rectangle. Its eastern boundary is dented by the curves of the Delaware River, and its northwestern corner stretches upward to

Pennsylvania is noted for its covered bridges, which span many of the state's numerous streams.

reach the shores of Lake Erie. Spreading over 45,302 square miles (117,332 square kilometers), it ranks thirty-third in area among the states.

Pennsylvania shares its western border with West Virginia and Ohio. New York is its northern neighbor, and New Jersey lies to the east, across the Delaware River. In the south, the Keystone State has common borders with Delaware, Maryland, and a corner of West Virginia. Called Mason and Dixon's Line for two surveyors who marked it in 1763, the 250-mile (647-kilometer) Pennsylvania-Maryland border has traditionally been regarded as the boundary between the northern and southern states.

Tens of millions of years ago, most of the land we now know as Pennsylvania was part of a vast inland sea. Gradually the water receded, exposing an oozing swamp where dense vegetation took root. Time after time the water seeped back, only to ebb slowly away. The pressure of the returning seas upon tons of dead and decaying plants and animals formed Pennsylvania's valuable deposits of fossil fuel—coal and petroleum.

The Hyner Vista is a breathtaking view of the West Branch of the Susquehanna River in Clinton County.

After the water disappeared for the final time, a slow but tremendously powerful movement of the earth's crust began in the northwest. The land creased and buckled into a series of mountain ridges running roughly from northeast to southwest. Great glaciers ground their way south from the Arctic, shearing off the peaks of the mountains and strewing rocks and boulders as finishing touches to the landscape.

Today, most of northern and western Pennsylvania belongs to the great Appalachian Plateau that stretches from New York to Alabama. Referred to as the Allegheny Plateau in Pennsylvania, this region is scored with deep, narrow valleys and flat-topped mountains. Other mountains include the Poconos in the northeast, noted for their extraordinary beauty. The Blue Ridge Mountains rise in south-central Pennsylvania and extend south to Georgia.

Pennsylvania has only two small areas that are relatively flat. The Piedmont, a narrow band of fertile lowlands running from New Jersey to Alabama, spans a portion of south-central Pennsylvania. This region includes York and Lancaster counties,

In the spring, wildflowers
such as bloodroot (left)
and hepaticas (right),
brighten the state's forests.

which boast some of the most productive farmland in the nation.
At the diagonally opposite corner of the state, along the shores of
Lake Erie, lies a narrow strip of low land that was once part of the
lake bed itself. Its rich sandy soil is excellent for the cultivation of
grapes.

THE FORESTS

Although Pennsylvania is one of the nation's most heavily
industrial states, about three fifths of its land is covered with
forests. With a national forest, 20 state forests, and 114 state parks,
Pennsylvania has more publicly owned forestland than all of the
other northeastern states combined.

Evergreens such as pine and hemlock cloak the mountains,
interspersed with beech, maple, birch, and other hardwoods.
Hickory, oak, and black walnut trees flourish in the valleys and
lowlands. In the spring, hepaticas, anemones, bloodroots, and
dog's-tooth violets paint the woods.

White-tailed deer can be spotted along highways and back roads
throughout the state. Pennsylvania's forests are also home to the
black bear, raccoon, opossum, skunk, red fox, and bobcat. The

ruffed grouse, Pennsylvania's state bird, is prized by hunters. Many fishermen dream of battling the giant muskellunge that inhabits some lakes and rivers. However, they are more likely to land sunfish, yellow perch, pickerel, bass, or brook trout.

LAKES AND RIVERS

If a pail were emptied at the top of Headwaters Mountain in Potter County, the water would reach three distinct destinations. Some would run northwest into Lake Erie and pass through the St. Lawrence Seaway to the Atlantic Ocean. Some would tumble south and flow down the Susquehanna River to Chesapeake Bay. The rest would roll to the Allegheny River, which would carry it to the Ohio and from there down the Mississippi to the Gulf of Mexico. Providing access to the Great Lakes, the Atlantic Ocean, and the Mississippi River system, Pennsylvania's waterways have been a major factor in shaping the history of the state.

Some 45,000 miles (72,420 kilometers) of rivers and streams wind across Pennsylvania, comprising three major river systems. The Delaware forms the state's eastern boundary and is a major avenue for shipping. Among its tributaries are the Schuylkill and the Lehigh. The broad, shallow Susquehanna crosses the central portion of the state on its course from New York to the Chesapeake. It is fed by the Juniata and the West Branch. In the west, the Allegheny and the Monongahela (locally known as the Mon) merge to form the Ohio.

Some 256 tiny ponds and natural lakes dot Pennsylvania. The largest, Lake Conneaut in the northwest, measures only 1.5 miles (2.4 kilometers) across. However, several man-made bodies of water are considerably larger. The Pymatuning Reservoir, which lies on the Pennsylvania-Ohio border, covers 26 square miles

(67 square kilometers). One of the state's most popular resorts, Lake Wallenpaupack in the Poconos, was created as a reservoir for a hydroelectric plant in 1927.

CLIMATE

The lowlands of southeastern Pennsylvania are generally warmer than the rest of the state, and can count on a longer growing season. January temperatures average 26 degrees Fahrenheit (minus 3.3 degrees Celsius) in the northern mountains and 34 degrees Fahrenheit (1.1 degrees Celsius) in the Philadelphia area. In July, the average temperature in the north is 70 degrees Fahrenheit (21.1 degrees Celsius), compared with 77 degrees Fahrenheit (25 degrees Celsius) in the southeast.

Extremes of temperature are not unknown in Pennsylvania. On January 5, 1904, the mercury plunged to a record low of minus 42 degrees Fahrenheit (minus 41.1 degrees Celsius) at Smethport. At Phoenixville on July 9 and 10, 1936, temperatures soared to 111 degrees Fahrenheit (43.9 degrees Celsius).

Annually, Pennsylvania receives an average of 42 inches (about 107 centimeters) of precipitation, including rain, sleet, and snow. Heavy rains sometimes cause flooding when rivers overflow their banks. The most catastrophic flood in Pennsylvania's history killed 2,200 people in Johnstown in 1889. In 1936, severe floods devastated large sections of Pittsburgh. The people of Wilkes-Barre, Sunbury, and other towns along the Susquehanna still shudder when they recall the flood of 1972, which destroyed millions of dollars in property and claimed dozens of lives.

Today, dams and floodgates help to reduce the number and severity of Pennsylvania's floods. But in a state crisscrossed with rivers, flooding is an enemy that can never be totally conquered.

Chapter 3

THE PEOPLE

THE PEOPLE

At five in the morning, the streets of downtown Lancaster echo with the rumble of wagon wheels and the clop-clop of horses' hooves as Amish farm families bring their produce to market. Men with flowing beards and women in bonnets and aprons sell garden-fresh lettuce, spinach, cucumbers, mounds of golden apples and peaches, homemade pies, sausage, scrapple, and cheese. In a world that is constantly changing, the Amish remain faithful to traditional ways that date back more than two hundred years.

Not far from the Amish market, on the outskirts of Lancaster, modern shopping malls lie adrift in a sea of parking lots. Families from the city examine the latest fashions and the most-popular record albums, eager to keep up with the times.

The Keystone State is a study in contrasts. From the Amish farmers of Lancaster County to the corporate chiefs of Pittsburgh, the people of Pennsylvania bring to their state a fascinating diversity.

POPULATION AND POPULATION DISTRIBUTION

According to the 1990 census, Pennsylvania ranks fifth among the states in population, with 11,881,643 people. Some 69 percent of all Pennsylvanians live in cities or suburbs. The remainder live on farms or in small towns.

Pennsylvania has two major centers of population—
Philadelphia and Pittsburgh. Philadelphia, on the Delaware River,
is the state's largest city and the fourth-largest city in the nation.
About one third of Pennsylvania's population is concentrated in
the Philadelphia metropolitan area. Pittsburgh, strategically
situated at the forks of the Allegheny, Monongahela, and Ohio
rivers, is the economic and cultural hub of western Pennsylvania.

Like Philadelphia and Pittsburgh, many other Pennsylvania
cities grew up along crucial waterways. Erie, the third-largest city
in the state, was built on the shore of Lake Erie and gives
Pennsylvania access to the Great Lakes. Allentown and Bethlehem
lie along the Lehigh River, and Altoona is near the Juniata.
Harrisburg, the state capital, began as a ferry port on the east bank
of the Susquehanna.

Pennsylvania also has extensive rural areas. Every resident of
the state lives within a few miles of a state park or forest.

WHO ARE THE PENNSYLVANIANS?

The 1980 census revealed that Pennsylvania had a larger
percentage of native-born residents than any other state. In an era
when people move from one state to another with each new shift
in the job market, Pennsylvanians of every ethnic background
have a special attachment to their roots.

By the outbreak of the American Revolution, Pennsylvania was
already a patchwork of ethnic enclaves. In the east lived English,
Welsh, French, Swedish, Finnish, and Dutch colonists. About one
third of the population was of German stock. Scotch-Irish families
had settled along the western frontier. Many blacks, both slaves
and freedmen, lived in and near Philadelphia, and American
Indians were scattered throughout the colony.

In the middle of the nineteenth century, thousands of Irish immigrants settled in Pennsylvania's cities and mining towns. Newcomers from Italy, Hungary, Poland, Lithuania, and Czechoslovakia poured into the state after the 1880s. In the twentieth century, the black population rose as families from the rural South migrated to northern cities in search of jobs. Most of these groups have melted into the American mainstream. Yet the people commonly called the Pennsylvania Dutch still cherish their unique traditions and maintain a distinct identity.

THE PENNSYLVANIA DUTCH

Brochures for tourists often refer to Lancaster County in south-central Pennsylvania as "Pennsylvania Dutch country." Actually, the "Pennsylvania Dutch" originally came from Germany rather than The Netherlands. The term "Dutch" derives from their word *Deutsch*, meaning German. Though Pennsylvania Germans live chiefly in Lancaster, York, Berks, and Dauphin counties, small communities are scattered throughout the state.

Many Pennsylvania Germans belong to one or another of the "Plain Sects," Protestant groups that emphasize simplicity in worldly matters. The Plain Sects include the Mennonites, Swenkfeldians, Moravians, Amish, and Brethren of Christ, sometimes called Dunkers. Though all of these groups are conservative, the Amish are the most deeply committed to their traditional way of life.

From the road, it is easy to recognize an Amish farmhouse, for no telephone wires link it to the outside world. Electricity, the telephone, and the automobile have no place in Amish life. Amish farmers still cultivate their fields with horse-drawn plows, and on Sunday mornings families ride in black buggies to church services.

Amish farmers
still cultivate
their fields
with horse-drawn
plows and harvest
wheat by hand.

Amish life has few frills, but the close-knit community offers support and security to its members. If a farmer's barn burns down, families from miles around turn out for a barn-raising.

RELIGION

Pennsylvania was founded by William Penn, a member of the Society of Friends, or Quakers, who firmly believed that people of all religious persuasions should have the freedom to worship. Thus, from the earliest colonial days, Pennsylvania has seen a peaceful blending of many faiths. Quakers, French Huguenots, Lutherans, members of the Plain Sects, Jews, and Roman Catholics all had a foothold in the colony by the middle of the eighteenth century.

Today, more than half of all Pennsylvanians are Roman Catholics. The state's major Protestant groups include Lutherans, Methodists, and Presbyterians. Though the Quakers are now a small minority in Pennsylvania, the Society of Friends still maintains its American headquarters in Philadelphia. Pennsylvania's Jewish population is concentrated chiefly in and around Philadelphia and Pittsburgh.

Chapter 4

THE BEGINNING

THE BEGINNING

In 1971, amateur archaeologist Albert Miller found a long flake of stone in a groundhog hole on his land north of Washington. The stone flake proved to be an ancient cutting tool. The site Miller had discovered, called the Meadowcroft Rock Shelter, preserves traces of the earliest known inhabitants of Pennsylvania, who lived there some twelve thousand years ago.

The stone tools, bits of pottery, and pieces of charcoal left by Pennsylvania's early hunters and gatherers offer few glimpses into their daily lives. Our most detailed knowledge about the Indians who lived here comes from the written records of European explorers who met them in the seventeenth century.

THE INDIANS

"They let it be understood that they are a free people, subject to no one, but do what they please." In these words, Swedish colonist Johann Printz described the Lenape, the people he encountered when he reached Pennsylvania in 1643. In scattered villages along the Delaware and Brandywine rivers, the Lenape lived in round huts of branches plastered with mud. The women planted corn and squash, and the men hunted for game in the forests. A peace-loving people, the Lenape were sometimes invited to settle disputes among neighboring tribes.

On the shores of the river that recalls their name today lived the Susquehannocks. Several Susquehannock families usually shared a single "long house," partitioned into rooms. English sea captain John Smith was impressed by their height and bearing.

The Monongahela people of western Pennsylvania built their villages on hilltops surrounded by sturdy log fences. Their beautifully carved pipes and intricate pottery demonstrate that they were excellent craftsmen. The Monongahelas disappeared mysteriously around the middle of the seventeenth century, perhaps due to a series of disastrous epidemics.

Two other tribes that occupied Pennsylvania were the Shawnee and the Erie. The Shawnee migrated to Pennsylvania from Kentucky and North Carolina in the early 1600s, and settled in the Ohio Valley. The Erie, who lived along the southern shore of Lake Erie, may have used poison-tipped arrows in hunting and warfare. By 1655, this group had been wiped out in a war with the powerful Iroquois of present-day New York State.

About fifteen thousand Indians lived in Pennsylvania in 1600. By 1790, only about one thousand remained. The coming of the first pale-skinned strangers from across the ocean spelled the destruction of the Indians' way of life.

THE FIRST EUROPEANS

By the early 1600s, many European nations vied for claims in the vast wilderness that was the New World. A Dutch explorer, Cornelius Mey, was probably the first white man to set foot on Pennsylvania soil, when he sailed into the lower reaches of the Delaware in 1614. The following year a Frenchman, Etienne Brulé, crossed Pennsylvania as he traced the course of the Susquehanna.

Swedish fur traders established the first European settlement in Pennsylvania in 1638, near present-day Philadelphia. During the next few years, more Swedish trading posts sprang up along the

In 1615, French explorer Etienne Brulé crossed Pennsylvania as he traced the course of the Susquehanna River (above).

Delaware. In 1643, Johan Printz arrived to act as governor of the region optimistically named New Sweden.

In 1655, Peter Stuyvesant, governor of Holland's New Amsterdam Colony, sent seven hundred men to lower the Swedish flags along the Delaware. The brief era of New Sweden was over, but Dutch control in Pennsylvania was even more short-lived. In 1664, a British military force drove the Dutch from New Amsterdam and stripped them of their Delaware River claims. The land now known as Pennsylvania was in British hands.

THE HOLY EXPERIMENT

British Admiral William Penn dreamed that his son would launch a career in politics. But young William was more interested in religion. In 1667, when he was twenty-three, Penn joined the Society of Friends, or Quakers. The Quakers felt that worship should be as simple as possible, and believed that warfare was a sin against God. Only the Anglican Church was sanctioned by the

HATHAWAY HIGH
1511

William Penn

Hannah Penn, William's wife

British government, and Quakers were often imprisoned for their beliefs. Penn dreamed of founding a colony in the New World where Quakers could worship freely.

King Charles II owed Admiral Penn eighty thousand British pounds. In 1681, to settle this debt, the king made young William Penn proprietor of more than 45,000 square miles (116,550 square kilometers) of land west of the Delaware River. King Charles named this land for the admiral, calling it Penn's Woods, or Pennsylvania. The territory encompassed nearly all of present-day Pennsylvania, plus three "lower counties" that separated to become the Delaware Colony in 1701.

To Penn, the governorship was an opportunity to put his religious ideals into practice. Before setting sail, he wrote, "There may be room there, though not here, for such a holy experiment."

In October 1682, the three-masted schooner *Welcome* sailed into the Delaware River, and Penn caught his first glimpse of the land he would govern. Endless forests stretched away from the

26

William Penn supervising the plans for Philadelphia, which he envisioned as
a city of parks

riverbank, but here and there Swedish, Finnish, and Dutch settlers
had cleared plots of land and built sturdy log cabins. Penn's
surveyors had already laid out a town on a spot between the
Schuylkill and the Delaware that afforded an excellent harbor.
Following Penn's instructions to create "the air of a country
town," they set aside land for four spacious city parks, a central
market, and a town hall. To name this new city, Penn chose a
Greek term that meant "City of Brotherly Love"—Philadelphia.

Believing that "we must give the liberties we ask," Penn
promised religious freedom to people of any faith that accepted
Almighty God as the Creator. Quakers and other religious
dissenters from England and Wales flocked to the colony. They
were followed by French Huguenots, Mennonites from Germany,
and refugees from a series of bloody European wars. Thousands of
men and women paid for their passage to the colony by

Dreaming of a lasting peace, Indian leaders gathered in Philadelphia and pledged their friendship with William Penn and his people.

contracting to serve a master for seven years or more. During their bondage, these "indentured servants" were little more than slaves.

The Indians of Pennsylvania believed in a Great Spirit that had made the earth and the sky. Penn concluded that this Great Spirit was the same God worshiped by Christians, and insisted that the Indians must be treated fairly. Settlers were forbidden to seize Indian land by force, and instead had to pay a just price for it. In 1701, leaders of the Susquehannock, Shawnee, and several other tribes gathered in Philadelphia and pledged lasting friendship with William Penn and his people.

When Penn arrived in 1682, scarcely five hundred Europeans lived in Pennsylvania. By 1700, the white population had soared to twenty thousand. Philadelphia was a thriving trading center, and farms flourished on the surrounding lowlands. People from half a dozen nations lived and worked side by side, and all were free to worship as they pleased. It seemed that Penn's holy experiment was a stunning success.

TRIUMPHS AND TROUBLES

After William Penn's death, his three sons became the joint proprietors of Pennsylvania. They had little interest in the colony. While they basked in luxury at court in London, the colonists went about their business, unhampered by British authority.

In 1723 a seventeen-year-old printer's apprentice named Benjamin Franklin ran away from his master in Boston and escaped to Philadelphia. One of the greatest geniuses America has ever produced, he became a leading writer, inventor, and diplomat. Franklin used much of his energy and talent to improve his adopted city, where he would spend most of the next sixty-seven years.

In 1731, Franklin helped to establish the Free Library of Philadelphia, the first circulating library in the colonies. He founded America's first volunteer fire department in 1736, and in 1752 established the first fire insurance company, known for its logo as the Hand in Hand. Other Philadelphians also made enduring civic improvements. Dr. Benjamin Rush established the first hospital in the colonies in 1751, and the first medical school in 1756. Botanist John Bartram created a dazzling public garden with plants from all over the world.

Many of the settlers in the Schuylkill Valley came from iron-producing regions of Wales and Germany, and they recognized the reddish deposits of iron ore in the Pennsylvania hills. The first ironworks opened at Coventry in Chester County in 1718, and by 1759, Pennsylvania led the colonies in iron production. Blacksmiths hammered out nails and axe blades, kettles and plowshares.

While the Europeans prospered, the Indians steadily lost ground. No natural immunity protected them from smallpox, measles, tuberculosis, and other diseases the white settlers brought from Europe, and epidemics devastated the tribes. Year by year, the settlers bought up the Indians' land, pushing them ever farther to the west. In 1737, the Indians were persuaded to sell yet another strip of land, its size to be based on the distance a man could walk in a day and a half. The whites prepared for this "walking purchase" by clearing paths through the forest, and the walkers covered far more ground than the Indians meant to sell. Their outrage at this trickery ushered in a thirty-year era of intermittent fighting between Indians and settlers.

Gradually, English and Scottish settlers pushed westward across the Allegheny Plateau. They were dismayed when, in 1753, two thousand French troops landed on the shore of Lake Erie and established forts at Presque Isle, Erie, and Le Boeuf (present-day Waterford).

The peace-loving Quakers who controlled the colonial assembly in Philadelphia were reluctant to take military action. Governor Dinwiddie of Virginia finally ordered the French to withdraw. In October 1753, Dinwiddie sent twenty-one-year-old Major George Washington to Fort Le Boeuf with the politely worded message, "It becomes my duty to require your peaceful departure." Just as politely, the French refused to budge, plunging the colonies into the long and bitter French and Indian War. The conflict spread to Europe, where it was called the Seven Years' War.

By the outbreak of the war, the French had erected another stronghold, Fort Duquesne, at the strategic forks of the Allegheny, Monongahela, and Ohio rivers. In 1755, British General William Braddock crossed the Alleghenies to attack the fort, but was disastrously defeated by the French and their Indian allies. By 1758, however, the tide turned against the French. Knowing themselves defeated, they blew up Fort Duquesne and fled from

British General William Braddock was shot in the lungs during his disastrous attack on Fort Duquesne in 1755 and died two days later.

Pennsylvania. Almost immediately, the British built Fort Pitt upon the ruins. In the decades to come, Fort Pitt evolved into the city of Pittsburgh.

Though the French had been driven from Pennsylvania, fighting continued between the colonists and the Indians. In 1763, Chief Pontiac of the Hurons to the north organized several tribes to launch a massive attack against the whites. In Pennsylvania they captured Forts Presque Isle and Le Boeuf, and held Fort Pitt under siege. When Swiss adventurer Henry Bouquet led a British force to relieve Fort Pitt, he was ambushed by Indians at Bushy Run, about twenty miles (thirty-two kilometers) from his destination. Bouquet pretended to retreat, but when the Indians pursued he turned on them in a surprise attack. Most of the Indians were killed, and the survivors scattered. The Battle of Bushy Run marked the last Indian resistance to white settlement in Pennsylvania, and the tragic end to Penn's dream that whites and Indians would live together in peace.

31

Chapter 5

THE STRUGGLE FOR INDEPENDENCE

THE STRUGGLE FOR INDEPENDENCE

"My God, that has given [this country] to me . . . will, I believe, bless and make it the seed of a nation," wrote William Penn in 1681. A century after he wrote these prophetic words, Pennsylvania stood at the tumultuous center of a revolution that would forge an independent nation from thirteen British colonies.

TAXATION WITHOUT REPRESENTATION

Under the loose proprietorship of William Penn's sons and grandsons, the people of Pennsylvania were relatively free to govern themselves. But when the Seven Years' War emptied England's treasury, the mother country turned to her American colonies as an untapped source of revenue. In 1765 the British Parliament passed the Stamp Act, which taxed newspapers, legal documents, and even decks of playing cards. The people of Pennsylvania were outraged. When a ship carrying British stamps anchored in Philadelphia Harbor, Philadelphians dressed in mourning as a protest.

Parliament finally repealed the Stamp Act, but soon replaced it with a fresh series of taxes under the Townshend Acts. Pennsylvanians felt that Parliament had no right to tax them. In 1768, the Pennsylvania Assembly sent a message to Parliament, calling for "no taxation without representation." But the message went unheeded.

BREAKING THE TIES

"The cause of one is the cause of all," wrote Pennsylvania statesman John Dickinson in 1768. Until the 1760s, the colonies had little sense of unity. But their grievances against the British drew them together. At last, leaders from most of the colonies agreed the time had come for united action.

Its central location made Philadelphia the ideal site for the First Continental Congress, which met at Carpenters' Hall on September 5, 1774. Delegates to the Congress from twelve colonies (Georgia was not represented) voted to boycott British imports "until all obnoxious acts shall be repealed."

By the time the Second Continental Congress convened at the Pennsylvania State House in May 1775, a more-radical climate prevailed. Three weeks before, colonial blood had been shed at Lexington and Concord in Massachusetts. A young Philadelphian named Thomas Paine was circulating a pamphlet entitled *Common Sense*, in which he said that "the sun never shone on so great and worthy a cause" as American independence.

In June, the Congress appointed George Washington as commander-in-chief of the Continental army. Thomas Jefferson, a delegate from Virginia, wrote a declaration stating that the colonists were no longer subject to British rule. Using the term *United States of America* for the first time, it declared that the states were to be independent of the crown. Benjamin Franklin helped strengthen the wording of this Declaration of Independence, which Jefferson presented to Congress on July 2.

The declaration aroused a storm of controversy in the Congress. The delegates voted on each contested line, and eliminated about one-third of the original document. On July 2, a majority of the delegates endorsed the resolution of independence presented by

Thomas Jefferson (standing) submitted his draft of the Declaration of Independence to Benjamin Franklin (left) and John Adams (center), who suggested some changes. Congress made further changes, shortening the original by about one third, before the majority of delegates signed the document on July 4, 1776.

Richard Henry Lee of Virginia. At last, on the evening of July 4, 1776, the amended Declaration was approved without dissent and was signed by John Hancock as president. The Declaration of Independence was first publicly proclaimed in Philadelphia at noon on July 8. On July 9, the Declaration was read to Washington and his troops in New York City. On July 19, Congress resolved to have the document "engrossed on parchment" for the signatures of the delegates, and on August 2, most of the fifty-six signatures were affixed. From the signers came two presidents, three vice-presidents, ten United States congressmen, nineteen illustrious jurists, and sixteen governors. In its final form, the Declaration is entitled "The Unanimous Declaration of the Thirteen United States of America."

Ever since the great bell in the tower of the State House pealed the news across Philadelphia, it has been revered as the Liberty

This Quaker farmhouse, located in Brandywine Battlefield State Park at Chadd's Ford, served as headquarters for the Marquis de Lafayette, French aide to General Washington, during the ill-fated Battle of Brandywine Creek.

Bell. The Pennsylvania State House, where the Continental Congress met, is known to this day as Independence Hall.

THE PRICE OF FREEDOM

When news of the Declaration of Independence reached London, Parliament determined to crush the rebellion. Within weeks, British warships patrolled Delaware Bay in an effort to blockade Philadelphia. In September 1777, British general Sir William Howe defeated George Washington's forces at the Battle of Brandywine Creek. Ten days later, some three hundred American soldiers died in the bloody Paoli Massacre.

The historic Battle of Germantown is reenacted each year at Clivedon.

British troops surged into Philadelphia, but George Washington launched a daring plan to win back the city. On October 4, Washington's forces assailed the key British position at Germantown just north of Philadelphia. An American victory was almost certain until a thick fog blanketed the battlefield. Confused by the poor visibility, colonial general Nathaniel Greene accidentally ordered his men to fire on a neighboring American column. Fearing themselves surrounded, the Americans broke ranks in a chaotic retreat.

As soon as Philadelphia fell to the British, the Continental Congress fled the city—first to Lancaster, and finally to York across the Susquehanna. To prevent the British from seizing valuable metal and other supplies, the colonists hastily loaded seven hundred wagons with goods, which they hauled to safety in Allentown and Bethlehem. The State House bell was hidden beneath the floorboards of an Allentown church.

While the British in Philadelphia enjoyed an elegant season of parties, balls, and theatricals, George Washington encamped his army at Valley Forge, eighteen miles (twenty-nine kilometers) from the city. The poorly fed, ill-equipped men built log huts for

Washington with his troops on the march to Valley Forge in December 1777

shelter. Supplies of bread and meat were irregular and the men often received their nourishment from "fire cake," a mixture of flour and water. Clothing, too, was inadequate, and the army was ravaged by sickness and disease.

The soldiers had been trained, but not uniformly. In February, Prussian military expert Baron Friedrich von Steuben arrived and worked tirelessly to train and drill the regiments into an effective fighting force.

As winter passed, the army underwent a dramatic transformation. Increasing amounts of supplies and equipment came into camp. New troops arrived. The training instilled new confidence in the men.

Spring brought word of the French alliance with its guarantee of military support. On May 6, a grand celebration marked the formal observance of the treaty.

Prussian military expert Baron Friedrich von Steuben worked tirelessly to train and discipline Washington's troops at Valley Forge.

Six months after its arrival, a strong, dependable, and well-trained American army departed Valley Forge to successfully engage the British at Monmouth, New Jersey.

A few months after France entered the war, the British abandoned Philadelphia to strengthen their forces in New York. But bloodshed in Pennsylvania was not yet at an end. In July 1778, some eight hundred British troops and their Iroquois allies traveled down the Susquehanna to attack the scattered American settlements in the Wyoming Valley. The terrified settlers took shelter in a fort near present-day Wilkes-Barre. In the battle known today as the Wyoming Massacre, about two thirds of the settlers died, many of them women and children.

As soon as the British left Philadelphia, Congress returned to the State House. On July 9 it approved the Articles of Confederation, a code of laws by which the liberated colonies would govern themselves.

In 1783, British and American leaders met in Paris to sign a treaty of peace. The long revolutionary war was over at last. The former British colonies had finally won their freedom.

THE UNITED STATES CONSTITUTION

It was clear that the Articles of Confederation were too weak and confusing to hold the new nation together. In the summer of 1787, delegates from each of the thirteen states met in Philadelphia to revise and strengthen the Articles.

George Washington presided over the series of meetings remembered today as the Constitutional Convention. The proceedings were cloaked in secrecy. The public was not aware of the debates that raged in the convention until Virginia statesman James Madison's private papers were published fifty years later.

One of the most crucial issues to be decided was how much voice each state should have in the central, or federal, government. The smaller states feared they would be dominated by the larger ones, while the large states thought it would be unfair for small states to have too much control. Benjamin Franklin, at eighty-one the convention's oldest delegate, pleaded for compromise. "When a broad table is to be made and the edges of planks do not fit, the artist takes a little from both and makes a good joint," he wrote. "In like manner here, both sides must part with some of their demands in order that they both join in some accommodating proposition." Finally, the delegates agreed on a bicameral, or two-house, Congress. Each state would elect representatives to the lower house, the number determined by the state's population. But regardless of population, every state would elect two senators to represent it in the upper house.

At last the delegates devised a body of laws, or Constitution,

After four months of debate during their meetings at Independence Hall in Philadelphia, delegates to the Constitutional Convention gathered to sign the final draft of the United States Constitution on September 17, 1787.

that created a strong central government, yet insured the sovereignty of the states as well. In December 1787, Pennsylvania became the second state to ratify the Constitution of the United States.

From 1790 until 1800, Philadelphia served as the capital of the new nation. It was also Pennsylvania's state capital until 1799, when the seat of government shifted to Lancaster. The state capital finally moved to its present location, Harrisburg, in 1812.

During its first few years, the new government scarcely touched the people of western Pennsylvania. Cut off from the rest of the state by rugged mountains, frontier society developed its own unwritten rules. Because roads across the mountains were almost

Violent clashes broke out during the "Whiskey Rebellion," when excise officers tried to collect taxes from western Pennsylvania distillers.

nonexistent, the farmers could not easily ship their grain to mills in the east. It was more profitable to convert much of the corn and rye they grew into whiskey, which could then be carried by boat to eastern markets. Whiskey came to be called "western money." It was sometimes even used instead of cash to pay workers' wages.

In 1791, Congress passed an excise tax—four cents to be paid on every gallon of distilled spirits produced in the United States. The tax was a direct threat to the whiskey-based economy of western Pennsylvania. Most of the farmers refused to register their stills with the government and violent clashes broke out when excise officers tried to collect the tax money. At last, in 1794, President George Washington ordered some fifteen thousand federal troops to march west and put down the insurrection. Vastly outnumbered, the farmers did not resist. The army rounded up several suspected leaders and took them back to Philadelphia, where they were tried for treason.

The "Whiskey Rebellion" had far-reaching implications for the nation as a whole. For the first time, the federal government had taken action to enforce one of its laws. The rebellion in western Pennsylvania served as a proving-ground for the authority of the United States government.

Chapter 6

FROM FRONTIER TO FACTORY

FROM FRONTIER TO FACTORY

"Boil the corn in clear water until the corn is soft and pulpy, and salt it to suit taste. This we called hulled corn. Then boil some good clean spring water and salt it a little. This we called water porridge or water broth. For breakfast we had hulled corn and water porridge. For dinner we had water porridge and hulled corn, and for supper we had for a change water broth and hulled corn. We all stood up very well and worked hard."

In 1817, when pioneer Chelsey Brockway and his family reached northwestern Pennsylvania, much of the Keystone State was still wild country. But vast changes loomed on the horizon. The nineteenth century transformed Pennsylvania from a land of untouched forests to one of the leading industrial states in the nation.

PENNSYLVANIA ON THE MOVE

For more than a century, poor transportation hindered Pennsylvania's development. In winter, dirt roads were slick with ice, and in the spring, they turned to sloughs of mud. Grain and other farm produce was often shipped to market in boats built to make only one trip, downstream. When they reached their destination, the farmers unloaded their goods, tore their boats apart, and made the long journey home on foot.

In 1794, work crews completed a 69-mile (111-kilometer) stone-surfaced road from Philadelphia to Lancaster. The most expensive

A Conestoga wagon train heads west in 1796 from the Spread Eagle Inn, a stop on the Old Lancaster Road.

construction project the nation had yet seen, the road cost nearly half a million dollars. To defray some of the cost, travelers paid tolls at gates, or pikes, along the road. The toll collector then turned the pike to let the traveler continue on his way. Thus the word "turnpike" refers to a toll road or highway. By 1832, more than 3,000 miles (4,828 kilometers) of turnpikes, as well as many toll-free roads, had been completed or were under construction in Pennsylvania.

Settlers and traders poured west across the Alleghenies. Many of them traveled in great blue and red painted wagons with arching canvas tops. These wagons were built by Germans in the town of Conestoga, near Lancaster. Pulled by teams of six horses, their harnesses jingling with bells, these Conestoga wagons could carry up to 3,500 pounds (1,588 kilograms) of goods. Sometimes caravans of fifty or more rumbled over Pennsylvania's newly made roads. Later, as settlers pushed the frontier across the Great Plains, the Conestoga wagon came to symbolize America's westward expansion.

In 1812, Robert Fulton's steamboat *New Orleans* chugged all the way from Pittsburgh to New Orleans.

In 1807, a Pennsylvanian named Robert Fulton built the first commercially feasible steam-powered boat. Five years later his steamboat *New Orleans* amazed the world by chugging all the way from Pittsburgh to New Orleans.

By the 1830s, a network of canals sprawled across Pennsylvania to link the state's major river systems. In addition, railroads had begun to transport freight and passengers. The first commercial railroad in the United States began operation in 1829 between Carbondale and Honesdale.

In 1800, the 300-mile (483-kilometer) journey from Philadelphia to Pittsburgh could take two to three weeks. With the advent of trains, steamboats, and canals, it was possible to reach Pittsburgh in an astonishing four days. Crucial to this journey was a remarkable feat of engineering called the Allegheny Portage Railroad, which bridged the gap between the western end of the Juniata Canal at Holidaysburg and the beginning of the next canal at Johnstown. Canal boats were placed on railroad cars

The Old Lemon House was an inn and station on the Allegheny Portage Railroad, which bridged the gap between canals at Holidaysburg and Johnstown and made it possible to reach Pittsburgh from Philadelphia in only four days.

and hauled over the mountains along a series of inclined planes that served as giant stairs.

These dramatic improvements in transportation opened Pennsylvania's frontier to land-hungry settlers. They also enabled Pennsylvania to supply some of the basic resources essential to a rapidly growing nation.

RAIDING NATURE'S STOREHOUSE

By the beginning of the nineteenth century, the dense forests around Philadelphia were almost gone, and Pennsylvanians could no longer rely on an inexhaustible supply of firewood. With the invention of an inexpensive coal-burning hearth in 1831, anthracite, or hard coal, became a crucial resource. Coal companies sent instructors to teach their customers how to use the new fuel, and anthracite was soon warming homes throughout the northeastern United States. Within a few years, hard coal fueled eastern Pennsylvania's iron forges.

Soft, or bituminous, coal became as important in western Pennsylvania as anthracite was in the east. Bituminous coal was converted into a hard, compact form called coke, which proved an ideal fuel for iron-smelting furnaces. Surrounded by enormous coal deposits, Pittsburgh developed as the hub of the iron-smelting industry.

In the mid-1840s, a young man named Samuel Kier began bottling the greasy black "rock oil" that oozed from salt wells near Torentum. He peddled his "Kier's Rock Oil" as a medicine to cure all ills. One of his advertisements ran:

> The beautiful balm from nature's secret spring,
> The bloom of health and life to man shall bring,
> As from her depths this magic fluid flows,
> To calm our suffering and assuage our woes.

Eventually, a bottle of Kier's Rock Oil reached a professor at Yale University. He concluded that, though it might not bring the bloom of health and life, it could be purified to make a fine fuel for lamps. In 1850, Kier opened the nation's first oil refinery at Pittsburgh to produce "carbon oil," or kerosene, for lighting.

In 1859, Edwin L. Drake invested his meager savings of two hundred dollars to drill for oil on the bank of Oil Creek near Titusville. After a discouraging series of cave-ins and broken pipes, Drake finally struck oil at a depth of sixty-nine feet (twenty-one meters). Gushing up through the pipe, the oil filled all of the whiskey barrels and washtubs the town could provide. Drake launched the nation's petroleum industry just as America hovered on the brink of a tragic civil war.

THE WAR BETWEEN THE STATES

The first recorded opposition to slavery in the American colonies was voiced by a group of Pennsylvania Germans in 1688. The Society of Friends also took a strong antislavery stand. The Quakers drafted an official statement condemning slavery in 1755, and barred slaveholders from attending their church services, or meetings. In 1780, Pennsylvania passed the first abolition law in the nation, declaring all black children born in the state to be free citizens.

As early as 1800, Quakers and free blacks in Pennsylvania began to help slaves escape from the South by means of the Underground Railroad. Runaway slaves were sheltered on their flight north in a series of "safe houses." Sympathetic farmers sometimes transported them in wagons beneath piles of corn or wheat. One slave, known as Henry "Box" Brown, reached the train station in Philadelphia nailed into a crate addressed to a local shoemaker. Although the crate was labeled THIS SIDE UP, WITH CARE, someone tossed it into the baggage car upside down, and Brown spent twenty-six hours standing on his head.

In the 1830s, a movement for the total abolition of slavery gained strength in the northern states, giving rise to the Republican party. Little by little, a dangerous gulf widened between the North and the South.

In 1861, the nation's newly elected Republican president, Abraham Lincoln, paused on his way to Washington and delivered a speech at Philadelphia's Independence Hall. "There shall be no bloodshed," he promised, "unless it be forced upon the government." Soon after Lincoln's inauguration, the southern states began to secede, or break away from, the United States. Convinced that Lincoln would make slavery illegal, they

The Battle of Gettysburg cost more human lives than any other battle fought in North America. Four months after the end of the Civil War, with his immortal Gettysburg Address, President Lincoln dedicated the Gettysburg National Cemetery.

determined to form a nation of their own — the Confederate States of America.

On April 15, Lincoln asked for volunteers to join the army that would fight to preserve the American Union. The young men of Pennsylvania rallied eagerly, filling twenty-five regiments within two weeks. But the excitement soon faded. As the lists of casualties grew longer, many Pennsylvanians questioned the wisdom of continuing the war effort.

In June 1863, Confederate commander Robert E. Lee led his army north into Pennsylvania. As Lee advanced, the Army of the Potomac remained between Lee and the capital to prevent Washington from being attacked. On July 1, the two armies met, almost by chance, on the outskirts of a sleepy college town called Gettysburg.

The Confederate army attacked that afternoon, and drove the Union troops to Cemetery Hill just south of the town. As the battle raged on through three brutal days, more Union troops rushed to Gettysburg to reinforce General George Meade's army. At last, twelve thousand Confederates under General George E. Pickett hurled themselves across an open field toward the center of the Union forces. Two thirds of the southern soldiers died in Pickett's Charge.

Both sides suffered catastrophic losses in the Battle of Gettysburg, but after Pickett's Charge, General Lee knew he was defeated. "It is I who have lost this fight," he told his weary men, "and you must help me out of it the best way you can." The Confederate army retreated back across the Potomac, leaving behind a battleground strewn with more than fifty thousand dead and wounded men. No other battle fought in North America has cost so many human lives.

Four months after the cannons fell silent, President Lincoln visited the battleground to dedicate the Gettysburg National Cemetery. Legend has it that Lincoln scribbled his speech on the back of an envelope while he rode the train from Washington. Actually, the speech went through two full drafts, but Lincoln still told a friend that it was "a flat failure." Yet the audience listened, spellbound, when he began his Gettysburg Address with the immortal words: "Fourscore and seven years ago. . . ."

Confederate troops invaded Pennsylvania once more before the Civil War came to an end. In July 1864, southern soldiers marched across Mason and Dixon's Line into Chambersburg. When the town council refused to hand over a supply of gold, the Confederates set a fire that destroyed two thirds of the town.

About 250,000 Pennsylvanians served their country during the course of the war. At last, in 1865, the Union and Confederate commanders signed a treaty of peace. After the long and bitter war, North and South were again one nation.

NEW INDUSTRIAL EMPIRES

In 1848, a thirteen-year-old boy named Andrew Carnegie left Scotland with his family and settled in Allegheny City, Pennsylvania, just outside Pittsburgh. To help with family expenses, young Andrew took a job as a bobbin boy in a textile mill. A few years later he worked for the Pennsylvania Railroad, and eventually he entered the iron business.

In 1873, Carnegie saw a demonstration of the newly developed Bessemer process for manufacturing steel. Steel was far stronger than iron, and Carnegie realized how valuable it would be in building bridges and locomotives. He opened steel plants at Braddock and Homestead, and was soon on his way to building an immense steel empire.

In 1901, Carnegie Steel merged with several other companies to form the vast United States Steel Corporation. When he retired, the former bobbin boy had amassed a fortune of nearly half a billion dollars. Andrew Carnegie used his wealth to endow schools and universities, to open public libraries across the country, and to champion the cause of world peace.

Among Carnegie's business associates were Henry Clay Frick and Charles Michael Schwab. Frick made a fortune manufacturing coke, and later became a director of U.S. Steel. Charles Schwab left U.S. Steel in 1903 to form the Bethlehem Steel Company on the Lehigh River.

Railroads were vital in the transportation of Pennsylvania's steel to markets throughout the country. The Pennsylvania Railroad and the Reading Railroad became two of the state's most powerful companies. Since coke was essential to fuel the steel furnaces, the coal industry, too, grew in tribute to the steel empires.

The booming steel, railroad, and coal industries became the backbone of Pennsylvania's economy. A few men grew wealthy, but thousands of workers, many of them recent European immigrants, struggled to feed their families.

While a few men became rich in the steel, railroad, and coal industries, thousands of workers struggled to feed their families. Most of Pennsylvania's laborers were recent European immigrants and their descendants. The first wave of newcomers reached Pennsylvania in the 1840s, when a terrible famine in Ireland drove thousands of desperate men and women to the United States in search of a better life. The 1880s and 1890s brought Poles, Hungarians, Slavs, Italians, and Jews. By 1900, no other state except New York had more foreign-born residents. The traditions of a dozen nations blended to change the texture of life in Pennsylvania forever.

Fleeing from the poverty they had known at home, the immigrants snatched at jobs in Pennsylvania's mines and factories. Wages were low, and working conditions were often treacherous. As they gained a firmer foothold in their adopted land, the immigrants fought to fulfill the promise of the American dream.

Chapter 7
PENNSYLVANIA COMES OF AGE

PENNSYLVANIA COMES OF AGE

"The rights and interests of the laboring man will be protected and cared for not by the labor agitators, but by the Christian men to whom God in His infinite wisdom has given control of the property interests of this country." Striking coal miners in Pennsylvania nicknamed this statement, made by management spokesman George F. Baer, the "Divine Right Letter." Feelings were passionate on both sides of the struggle between owners and workers, rich and poor, that thrust Pennsylvania into the twentieth century.

THE WORKERS UNITE

The roots of the American labor movement are planted deep in Pennsylvania's history. In 1791, Philadelphia carpenters staged the first "turn out," or strike, in the nation—to demand a twelve-hour working day. By the late 1800s, strikes occurred more frequently. Among the most violent were the 1891 Connellsville miners' strike, the 1892 Homestead steelworkers' strike, and the 1897 Luzerne County miners' strike. Workers in the railroad, steel, and coal industries organized to fight for higher wages, shorter hours, and safer conditions on the job.

Perhaps the most horrifying working conditions of all existed in Pennsylvania's anthracite mines. In the deep, narrow tunnels where the miners toiled with their picks and shovels, the air was thick with suffocating coal dust. Deadly fires, floods, cave-ins, and explosions were common. Between 1870 and 1900, 9,394 men died

By the late 1800s, workers in Pennsylvania's railroad, steel, and coal industries were organizing to fight for higher wages, shorter hours, and safer working conditions. Striking Pittsburgh railroad workers set fire to this B & O Railroad roundhouse in 1877.

in the mines—an average of two a day. As many as five miners a day were injured. "Breaker boys," who spent their days picking bits of coal from bins of slag, were often as young as eight or nine.

In 1898, a young labor organizer named John Mitchell urged the anthracite miners to forget their ethnic differences and unite for their common good. "The coal you dig isn't Slavish, Polish, or Irish coal," Mitchell declared. "It's coal." Gradually, Mitchell won a loyal following. In the spring of 1902, 150,000 anthracite workers quietly walked off the job. Under Mitchell's leadership, the strike remained peaceful through five long months.

Low pay, long hours, and dangerous working conditions led Pennsylvania anthracite miners and young "breaker boys" (left and above) to walk off their jobs in 1902. They returned to work only after the nation's supply of heating coal had begun to run out and President Theodore Roosevelt (above left) ordered the mine operators to submit to arbitration.

At last, as the nation's supply of heating coal sank to a dangerously low level, President Theodore Roosevelt ordered the mine operators to submit to arbitration. The owners granted the miners an eight-hour day and a 10 percent wage increase, and promised not to fire the men who had taken part in the strike.

Working conditions for miners and steel workers were still far from ideal. But John Mitchell's strike of 1902 brought a sense of hope to workers in the Keystone State and across the nation.

THE STRUGGLE FOR CHANGE

In 1906, President Theodore Roosevelt traveled to Harrisburg to dedicate Pennsylvania's new State Capitol. The building's magnificent green dome could be seen from every part of the city. Roosevelt called the new Capitol "the handsomest building I ever saw."

The Capitol symbolized Pennsylvania's commitment to change as the twentieth century got underway. In 1905 the state created a new Department of Health and Sanitation, which waged a tireless war against typhoid fever. In the same year, Pennsylvania passed some of the most innovative conservation laws in the country, establishing wildlife refuges and protecting black bears and female deer.

Nevertheless, the state government was in the grip of a ruthless political machine. Vast corporations bought the support of such Republican "bosses" as Boies Penrose, who in turn set tax policies that favored big business. One writer commented that the Standard Oil Company did "everything with the Pennsylvania Legislature except refine it."

When the United States plunged into the First World War, Pennsylvania's steel plants made a major contribution to the war effort. The Bethlehem Steel Company turned out warships and munitions, and Pittsburgh was sometimes referred to as the "arsenal of the nation." Thousands of black people from the South flocked to Pennsylvania's cities to take jobs in factories and war plants—a migration that continued for the next thirty years.

Campaigning for governor in 1922, a young Republican named Gifford Pinchot promised widespread social reform. When he was elected, Pinchot kept his word. He improved the treatment of the mentally ill, and worked to clean up polluted streams and rivers.

Unemployment during the Great Depression of the 1930s forced thousands of
Pennsylvania mining families to live in makeshift dwellings such as this.

Pledging to "get the farmers out of the mud," he paved thousands
of miles of roads in the state's rural areas. In spite of his increased
spending on public services, Pinchot managed to liquidate the
state's $20 million debt.

In spite of Pinchot's reforms, the Republican bosses clung to
their power in most parts of the state until the Great Depression
of the 1930s. Across the nation factories closed, farm prices
plummeted, and millions of people lost their jobs. In
Pennsylvania, unemployment in some mining and steel towns
soared to 80 percent. In the cities, soup kitchens struggled to feed
the starving families that lined up at their doors.

The voters blamed their Republican leaders for much of their
plight. In the election of 1932, they pinned their hopes on the
opposing Democratic party. For the first time in nearly sixty years,
the Democrats won a majority in the state legislature.

In 1932, Pennsylvania passed the Talbot Act to provide relief for
the unemployed. Further help came the following year with
President Franklin D. Roosevelt's New Deal. Federal money paid
thousands of Pennsylvanians to build schools, hospitals, and
roads. Conservation projects created state parks and built dams
for flood control.

The hardships of the depression did not truly come to an end, however, until the threat of another world war sent Pennsylvania's labor force back to work. Once again, coal and oil fields produced vital fuel, and the steel mills churned out munitions for the war effort. During World War II, Pennsylvania ranked second among the states in its manufacturing output, and seventh in the number of war contracts it received.

DREARY BLUE SKIES

During the early 1940s, gray skies hung over Pittsburgh like a banner, proclaiming its staggering steel production. Drivers often had to turn their headlights on at noon in the city so smoky it earned the nickname "hell with the lid taken off."

Pittsburgh and other manufacturing cities remained prosperous through the 1950s. But gradually, the state's glowing economic profile began to fade. By the early 1960s, the steel industry faced increasing competition from other states and from abroad. More and more workers were laid off, and once-bustling factories shut their doors. Between 1970 and 1980, Johnstown lost 29 percent of its jobs. Clear skies over Pittsburgh and other "smokestack" cities signaled hard times. As one worker put it, "when there ain't no smoke, there ain't no work. Now there ain't any smoke and there won't be any."

As factory jobs vanished, it was obvious that Pennsylvanians would have to prepare for new careers. Governor Richard Thornburgh, who served from 1979 until 1987, worked to attract industries that relied on highly advanced technology. Thousands of men and women found jobs in the computer, biotechnology, and telecommunications industries. A booming tourism industry opened additional opportunities. In the Poconos, in Bedford

Today, Pennsylvania's biotechnology, telecommunications, and computer industries employ thousands of former factory workers.

County on the Maryland border, and in the Laurel Highlands of the southwest, new jobs developed in hotels and ski resorts. By the mid-1980s, tourism had created as many jobs as the steel industry.

But the transition from a "smokestack" to a "high-tech" economy has not been an easy one. By 1986, some twenty-five thousand unemployed Pittsburgh steelworkers were still gazing in despair at the blue skies overhead.

QUESTIONS AND CHALLENGES

Early in the morning on March 28, 1979, residents of Middletown, just south of Harrisburg, woke to a shuddering roar. The truth of what had happened was almost as terrifying as the wild rumors that flashed through the once-peaceful communities along the Susquehanna. Vital equipment had malfunctioned at the Three Mile Island Nuclear Power Plant, triggering the worst commercial nuclear accident in the nation's history. Out of control, the plant spewed deadly radioactive steam over an area twenty miles (thirty-two kilometers) in diameter.

In the spring of 1979, the worst commercial nuclear accident in the nation's history occurred at the Three Mile Island Nuclear Power Plant in Middletown.

Fortunately, the plant's safety systems prevented any immediate deaths or injuries. But through the years that followed, many residents of Harrisburg and neighboring towns endured a nightmare of fears about the long-term effects of radiation exposure. "I just get the feeling we're all living on a time bomb," Louise Hardison of Londonderry Township told a reporter. "It's rotten. The whole thing is rotten." The accident at Three Mile Island spurred national debate over the safety of other reactors and the wisdom of using nuclear power at all.

The cleanup of Three Mile Island was only one of a daunting array of environmental problems that plagued Pennsylvania in the 1980s. Since 1962, an underground fire had smoldered in the abandoned anthracite mines beneath the town of Centralia, defying every effort to bring it under control. Chemical wastes from factories tainted once-sparkling rivers.

Gnawing problems confronted Pennsylvania's cities, too. As factories closed and businesses moved to the suburbs, unemployment within the cities climbed. Hardest hit were minorities, who generally had little voice in local government.

Substandard conditions existed in public housing, schools, and hospitals in minority sections of such cities as Pittsburgh and Philadelphia.

The morale of blacks rose in 1984 when the people of Philadelphia elected Wilson Goode, the first black mayor in the city's history. But in May 1985, tragedy marred Goode's administration. A radical group called Move, which believed in abolishing all existing laws, had established a commune in a working-class black neighborhood in West Philadelphia. Neighbors reported that the commune's children rummaged through garbage pails for food, and claimed that Move blared vulgar messages over a loudspeaker day and night.

City police ordered the Move members to vacate their house, but they barricaded themselves inside. At last the police dropped a firebomb from a helicopter onto the roof. The house became a blazing inferno, and the fire raced through the neighborhood, destroying sixty-one other homes. Eleven people died in the Move house, six of them children.

After an investigating commission found the mayor and his aides ''grossly negligent'' in the decision to drop the firebomb, Goode issued a formal apology. In a televised speech he declared, ''To say that I am sorry for the lives lost, for homes destroyed, for damage to our spirits somehow can never be enough.''

Yet Philadelphia's spirit has not been broken. In even the most impoverished neighborhoods, men and women work ceaselessly to build better lives for themselves and the people around them. In 1968 Sister Falaka Fatah and her husband turned their West Philadelphia row house into a home for teenaged boys who were in trouble with the law. By 1987, they had helped seven hundred boys stay in school and prepare for future jobs. The center they created is called Umoja—a Swahili word meaning unity.

Chapter 8

GOVERNMENT AND THE ECONOMY

GOVERNMENT AND THE ECONOMY

Every year, the people of Pennsylvania pay millions of dollars in taxes to the state government in Harrisburg. Officials chosen by the people determine how tax dollars will be spent. The state government provides an array of services including education, mass transit, and health care. Services rendered by the government are said to be in the public sector.

The private sector, on the other hand, consists of the profit-making companies and corporations that operate within the state. For Pennsylvania's economy to remain healthy, public and private sectors must function smoothly together.

GOVERNMENT

Pennsylvania is one of five states officially called a commonwealth, a term referring to a nation or state governed by the people. The Commonwealth of Pennsylvania has had five constitutions during its history. Under the current constitution, ratified in 1968, the government is divided into three branches. The legislative branch, or General Assembly, makes the laws. The judicial branch interprets these laws, and the executive branch, or office of the governor, carries them out.

Like the Congress of the United States, Pennsylvania's General Assembly is divided into two houses. Fifty members sit in the upper house, or senate, and 203 members are elected to the lower house, or house of representatives. Any member of the General Assembly may propose a new bill. After study and debate, the members vote to determine whether the bill should became a law.

The judicial branch of the government, or court system, resembles a vast pyramid. At the bottom are many small municipal and community courts. Each of the state's sixty-seven counties has a county court. Above these are sixty judicial districts, each with a court of common pleas. Cases may be appealed to the commonwealth court or to the superior court. At the top of the pyramid stands the state supreme court at Harrisburg. The seven supreme court justices are elected to ten-year terms.

The chief executive, or governor, is elected to a term of four years, and may serve only two terms in a row. The people also elect the lieutenant governor, state treasurer, attorney general, and auditor general. The governor appoints an adjutant general, secretary of the commonwealth, secretary of education, and several other officials.

About one-third of Pennsylvania's revenue comes from personal income tax, and another third is collected through sales and use taxes. A "use tax" is levied on certain goods bought outside the state but used in Pennsylvania. Other revenue comes from corporate taxes, inheritance taxes, a tax on real estate transfers, and some federal grants.

EDUCATION

Public education is the largest single expenditure in the Pennsylvania state budget. By law, all children between the ages of eight and sixteen must attend school. Approximately 2 million students are enrolled in public elementary and secondary schools,

Students at Penn Charter (center) attend a Quaker school that was founded in 1689 and those at the University of Pennsylvania's Wharton School (left) and Dickinson University (right) attend schools that were founded in the 1700s.

and another 400,000 attend private schools. MMI Preparatory School in Freeland, founded in 1879 as a school for the sons of miners and mechanics, is now a coeducational school that prepares students for college. Pennsylvania has a strong system of Catholic schools, and some fine Quaker schools operate in the Philadelphia area. The William Penn Charter School, or Penn Charter, founded by William Penn in 1689, is still open today.

Pennsylvania has more than 150 accredited two-year and four-year universities. In 1753, the Philadelphia Academy, founded by Benjamin Franklin, merged with the Charity School, eventually evolving into the University of Pennsylvania. The university's School of Medicine, which opened in 1765, is the oldest medical school in North America. The University of Pennsylvania is also noted for the Wharton School of Finance and Commerce, one of the nation's leading business schools.

Several other universities date back to the eighteenth century, including Dickinson at Carlisle (1773), Washington and Jefferson in Washington (1780), and the University of Pittsburgh (1787).

Students between classes enjoy the autumn sunshine on the campuses of Bryn Mawr (left) and the University of Pittsburgh (above).

The state is home to many excellent private colleges and universities, including Villanova, Haverford, Bryn Mawr, Swarthmore, Gettysburg, Allegheny at Meadville, Ursinus at Collegeville, and Bucknell University at Lewisburg. Temple and Drexel universities are other schools located in Philadelphia.

Pennsylvania State University, usually known as Penn State, is a sprawling complex of undergraduate and graduate schools located at twenty-two campuses across the state. The main campus in the town of State College originated in 1855 as the Farmers' High School. Students at Penn State can earn degrees in agriculture, architecture, business, education, engineering, geology, and liberal arts. The Pennsylvania State University of Medicine is located at Hershey.

Other state-funded universities in Pennsylvania include schools at Bloomsburg, Cheyney, Clarion, East Stroudsburg, Edinboro, Kutztown, Lock Haven, Mansfield, Millersville, Shippensburg, Slippery Rock, and West Chester. To the delight of trivia buffs, California State University and Indiana State University are both located in the Keystone State.

Forty-four Pennsylvania freight lines carry about one sixth of the nation's rail freight and more than 80 million vehicles use the Pennsylvania Turnpike each year.

TRANSPORTATION

With its ideal location, Pennsylvania is a leading center of shipping. Oceangoing vessels ply their way up Delaware Bay to Philadelphia, the world's largest freshwater port, 90 miles (145 kilometers) from the Atlantic. Erie is a key port for Great Lakes cargo ships. At the forks of the Allegheny, Monongahela, and Ohio rivers, Pittsburgh is a capital of inland shipping.

Though freight and passenger service by rail have declined in the United States, Pennsylvania still has 9,000 miles (14,484 kilometers) of railroad tracks in use. Passengers can reach thirty cities within the state by train. Forty-four freight lines carry about one sixth of the nation's rail freight.

In 1940, the first link of the Pennsylvania Turnpike, from Middlesex to Irwin, opened a new era for the American motorist. The first high-speed, multilane highway in the nation, the turnpike was completed in 1951. It spans southern Pennsylvania from Philadelphia to the Ohio border, with a branch extending north to Scranton. Toll-free Interstate 80 speeds cars and trucks across the northern portion of the state.

71

Pennsylvania's steel factories produce about a seventh of all the steel manufactured in the nation.

Pennsylvania has six international airports, served by twenty-seven foreign and domestic airlines. The largest airfields are in Philadelphia and Pittsburgh.

COMMUNICATIONS

The *American Weekly Mercury*, which began publication in Philadelphia in 1729, was Pennsylvania's first newspaper, and the first paper to appear in the colonies outside Boston. Today Pennsylvania has about 430 newspapers, 110 of them dailies. The *Philadelphia Inquirer* is the most widely read paper in eastern Pennsylvania. The *Pittsburgh Post-Gazette* and the *Pittsburgh Press* are leading papers in the west. The *Pittsburgh Courier* is one of the country's foremost black-oriented newspapers.

On November 2, 1920, radio station KDKA began broadcasting in Pittsburgh. With Detroit's WWJ, which went on the air on the same day, it was the nation's first commercial radio station. Today about 360 radio stations and 35 television stations are licensed to operate in Pennsylvania.

MANUFACTURING

Manufacturing accounts for about 87 percent of Pennsylvania's gross state product—that is, the total value of goods and services produced in the state. Despite a decline in the market, Pennsylvania still produces about an eighth of the pig iron and a seventh of the steel manufactured in the nation. Pittsburgh leads the state in steel production, but furnaces operate in Bethlehem, Erie, Harrisburg, Johnstown, Scranton, Steelton, and Wilkes-Barre as well.

Pennsylvania also produces nonelectric machinery such as air and gas compressors and tools and dies. Motors and generators, lighting equipment, semi-conductors, and other pieces of electrical equipment are also made in the state. A wide variety of processed foods are made and packaged in the Philadelphia area, including beer, baked goods, sausages, and luncheon meats. Other important Pennsylvania products include fabricated metals, chemicals, clothing, paper, and glass.

NATURAL RESOURCES

Though other fuels have largely replaced coal in home heating, about 40,000 Pennsylvanians were still working in coal fields in 1980. Pennsylvania ranks fourth in the nation in total coal production, and is the only source of anthracite in the country. Geologists estimate that about 35 billion short tons (32 billion metric tons) of coal still lie beneath Pennsylvania's soil—enough to meet the nation's energy needs for the next 350 years.

During the 1890s, Pennsylvania led the country in oil production. By the 1980s, however, the state's output of 4 million barrels a year accounted for only 1 percent of the oil produced in the United States. Refined at Marcus Hook, Oil City, Philadelphia, and Warren, most of Pennsylvania's petroleum is used for motor oil.

Natural gas, a by-product of Pennsylvania's oil fields, was once burned off as waste. Today, however, it is recognized as a clean, practical fuel. With an annual production of 195 billion cubic feet (5.5 billion cubic meters), Pennsylvania ranks among the leading producers of natural gas in the country.

Small but productive veins of iron ore, copper, and zinc are tapped by Pennsylvania's mines. Quarries produce slate, clay, sand, and limestone. The nation's largest processor of stone products, Pennsylvania converts raw slate to roofing tiles, clay to bricks, sand to window glass, and limestone to cement.

More than half of Pennsylvania's land is covered by forests, with millions of acres in the hands of commercial timber companies. The state's timber yield is valued at $5 billion a year. Among the most valuable trees are oak, maple, and pine. Black cherry, prized by makers of furniture for its rich color and lustrous grain, is sometimes called the crown jewel of Pennsylvania timber.

AGRICULTURE

FRESH CORN AND LOPES, proclaim the signs along the back roads of central Pennsylvania. Sooner or later most motorists give in to temptation, stopping to inspect the stacked ears of corn and mounds of "lopes," or cantaloupes, at one of the roadside stands. Though Pennsylvania is predominantly an industrial state, agriculture is a very important facet of the state's character.

About 40 percent of Pennsylvania's total farm income is derived from milk and dairy products. Most dairy farms are located in the

Though Pennsylvania is predominately an industrial state, agriculture is an important source of income.

eastern half of the state. Poultry farms are concentrated in Lancaster County, while beef cattle graze along the Susquehanna and in the rolling southwestern hills.

During the 1930s, farmers in Chester and Delaware counties experimented with raising mushrooms. Today Pennsylvania leads the nation in both mushroom production and canning. It is also the country's chief producer of cigar-leaf tobacco, most of it grown in Lancaster County. Corn, potatoes, hay, and wheat are among Pennsylvania's other vegetable crops. Apple and peach orchards stand in southeastern Pennsylvania. Adams County is noted for its sour cherries, and vineyards thrive along Lake Erie. Pennsylvania is the nation's leading supplier of commercially grown Christmas trees, most of them grown in Indiana County.

Averaging 148 acres (60 hectares) in size, most Pennsylvania farms are relatively small. But in an age when the family farm is being plowed under by agribusiness, Pennsylvania's small farms continue to flourish.

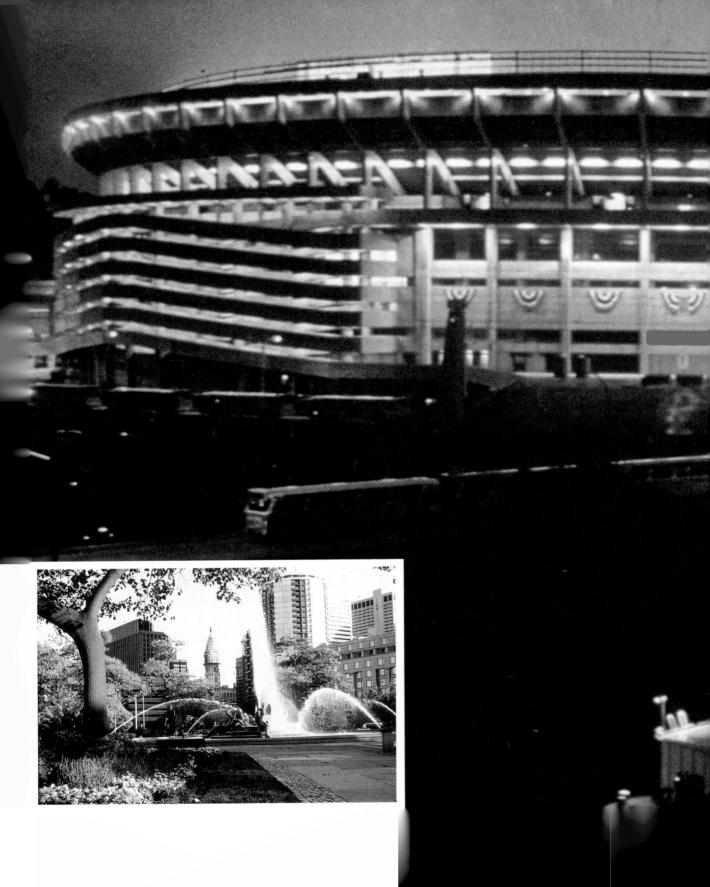

Chapter 9
ARTS AND LEISURE

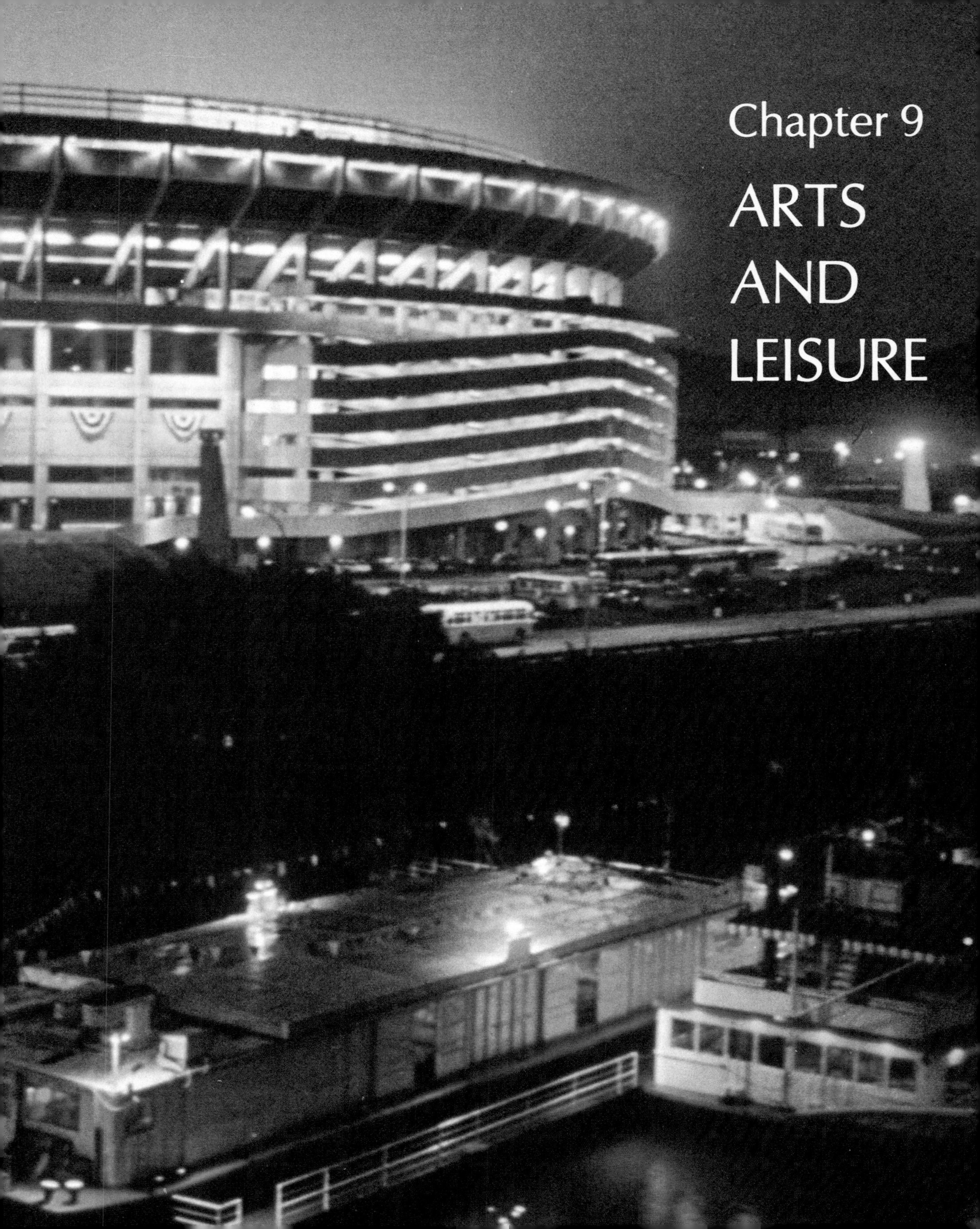

ARTS AND LEISURE

One of the best ways to understand the character of
Pennsylvania is to examine the artistic and athletic achievements
of its diverse people.

LITERATURE

Like modern advertisements such as "You Have a Friend in
Pennsylvania," the earliest writings produced in Pennsylvania
tried to entice European colonists to the new land. William Penn
painted a glowing picture of the colony in *Some Account of the
Province of Pennsylvania*. John Holme and Richard Frame, who
depicted the colony in verse, were Pennsylvania's first poets.

Among Benjamin Franklin's many talents was a flair for
writing. Franklin's autobiography furnishes a close-up view of his
work and personal life, and sheds light on the social and political
issues of early America. During his lifetime, Franklin gained
immense popularity with his *Poor Richard's Almanack*, published
annually from 1732 to 1757. The Almanack was a pocket-sized
book of jokes, stories, witty sayings, and advice to farmers. "Poor
Richard" is still remembered for such bits of wisdom as: "Fish
and visitors smell in three days," and "Early to bed, early to rise,
makes a man healthy, wealthy, and wise."

The first American ever to earn a living entirely by writing was
Philadelphia-born Charles Brockton Brown. Sometimes called the

Muckraking author Ida Tarbell (on the left, with her mother and sister) grew up in the family home in Titusville (left).

"father of the American novel," Brown specialized in tales of horror and suspense. In his most famous novel, *Wieland*, published in 1798, a mad ventriloquist hears mysterious voices that urge him to murder his family. Though Brown is seldom read today, he influenced many literary figures of the nineteenth century. Chief among them was Edgar Allan Poe, who worked as a magazine editor in Philadelphia between 1838 and 1844. A master of the macabre, Poe wrote some of his best-known horror stories, including "The Murders in the Rue Morgue," during his Philadelphia years.

By the late 1800s, a group of writers known as muckrakers used their literary skills to expose the excesses of the giant corporations. Born in Erie County, Ida Tarbell upheld the muckraking tradition with her scathing *History of the Standard Oil Company*. She also wrote biographies of Abraham Lincoln and Napoleon, and an autobiography, *All in the Day's Work*.

The twentieth century saw a flowering of literary talent in Pennsylvania. Christopher Morley of Haverford won national recognition for such novels as *Parnassus on Wheels* and *Kitty Foyle*. Critic Malcolm Cowley wrote about the "Lost Generation" of

Pennsylvania writers (left to right) John Updike, Malcolm Cowley, and Conrad Richter

American writers who lived in Paris during the 1920s. Born in Belsano, Cowley celebrated the beauty of the Juniata River country in his 1929 collection of poems, *Blue Juniata*.

Conrad Richter of Pine Grove set several of his novels in colonial Pennsylvania. In *The Light in the Forest* and *A Country of Strangers*, he portrays the conflicts of white children who were captured by Indians and brought up as members of an Indian tribe. Richter won the 1951 Pulitzer Prize in fiction with his novel *The Town*, and the 1961 National Book Award for fiction with *The Waters of Chronos*.

Throughout his work, John O'Hara criticized the shallowness he saw in middle-class American society. Many of his novels are set in the fictitious town of Gibbsville, Pennsylvania, modeled on O'Hara's native Pottsville. Works such as *Appointment in Samarra*, *Butterfield 8*, and *Ten North Frederick* shocked many readers when they first appeared.

Like O'Hara, John Updike reveals the darker side of American affluence. He, too, invents a small Pennsylvania town, Olinger, based on his hometown of Shillington. In *Rabbit Run* and its sequels, Updike traces the career of Rabbit Angstrom, a one-time high-school basketball star who struggles to accept the realities of

Portrait painter Charles Willson Peale (on the far left in Peale's family portrait) was among the many artists who studied at the London studio of Benjamin West (shown here in a self portrait).

everyday life. Though many of Updike's short stories and novels deal with the problems of families torn by divorce, his poetry reflects an underlying optimism about man's condition.

ART

The first Pennsylvanian to achieve widespread fame as an artist was Benjamin West. West was born in Springfield in 1738 to a devout Quaker family. Like most Quakers of their day, West's parents regarded art as an unnecessary frill, and forbade young Benjamin to paint. According to legend, he continued to paint in secret, making brushes with hairs he plucked from the family cat. Though West lived in London after 1763, many of his historical paintings, such as *Penn's Treaty with the Indians*, have American themes.

Among the many artists who studied for a time at West's London studio was portrait painter Charles Willson Peale. Peale was one of the founders of the Pennsylvania Academy of the Fine

The Boating Party **is a painting by artist Mary Cassatt, whose favorite subjects were women and children.**

Arts in Philadelphia, the first art college and museum in America. Convinced that virtually anyone could learn to paint if given proper training, Peale taught art to several of his seventeen children and to his brother James. James Peale, along with Charles's sons Raphaelle, Rembrandt, and Titian Ramsey, all became noted painters in their own right.

The work of Thomas Eakins is remarkable for its attention to realistic detail. Eakins studied painting at the Pennsylvania Academy of the Fine Arts. He also learned human anatomy at Philadelphia's Jefferson Medical College—the setting for his famous painting *In the Clinic of Dr. Gross*. Eakins' paintings of swimmers, rowers, and prizefighters recreate the beauty of the human body in motion.

Born in Pittsburgh, Mary Cassatt also studied at the Pennsylvania Academy of the Fine Arts. In 1868 she moved to Paris, where she spent the rest of her life. She modeled for many of the leading French Impressionist painters, especially Degas, while continuing to develop her own talent. Cassatt's finest paintings are sensitive portraits of women and children.

This mobile by sculptor Alexander Calder hangs in the National Gallery of Art in Washington, D.C.

Alexander Calder came from a family of Philadelphia artists. His mother was a painter, and his father, Alexander Milne Calder, sculpted the bronze figure of William Penn that crowns Philadelphia's City Hall. Trained as an engineer, Calder used his technical background to create intricate mobiles with carefully shaped sheets of metal hung on wires. Passing air currents keep the pieces in constant motion.

The influence of Thomas Eakins' realism is evident in the work of Andrew Wyeth. Born in Chadd's Ford near Philadelphia in 1917, Wyeth chooses rural Pennsylvania as the setting for many of his vividly detailed paintings. Perhaps the most popular American painter of the twentieth century, Wyeth lets his viewers look back to simpler, less troubled times.

Among the traditional
folk arts and crafts
of Pennsylvania Germans
are quilt making, hex
sign painting, and
furniture painting.

FOLK ART

The early arts and crafts of the Pennsylvania Germans are
delightfully colorful and creative. Bringing the tradition from
Germany, they applied brightly painted decoration to household
objects, using designs of flowers, birds, and geometric shapes.

Painted, patterned furniture offered color against the bare white walls of the settlers' homes. Typical pieces of decorated furniture were blanket or storage chests, Bible boxes, spice cupboards, wainscot chairs, and gate-legged tables.

Pottery was important in the daily life of the family. Almost every community had a redware potter who made plates, jars, and jugs. Some were left plain; others were decorated with incised bands or borders, then dried and glazed. In another form of pottery decoration, slip was used: a thick, white clay was trailed on the unbaked clay form and allowed to dry before being glazed. Though most designs were floral, some pieces were decorated with inscriptions, animals, or people.

The textiles of Pennsylvania Germans were unique. Woolen coverlets were woven in two strips on narrow looms and sewn together. Quilt making developed as a fine art in Pennsylvania and continues among some sects today. The quilting bee was a social event that brought women together for news and gossip.

A unique craft expression is the Pennsylvania Fraktur, or illuminated manuscript writing, that originated in medieval cloisters. Fraktur—heavy, black Gothic lettering—was used on certificates of birth and baptism, bookplates, and house blessings. Common motifs were stars, trees of life, goldfinches, and various floral designs, especially tulips, roses, and lilies.

Painted furniture, pottery, coverlets, quilts, and Fraktur are all part of the rich, colorful tradition of Pennsylvania folk art.

MUSIC

Perhaps America's best-loved composer of popular songs is Stephen Collins Foster, born in Lawrenceville (now part of Pittsburgh) in 1826. Though he never lived in the South and made only one visit below Mason and Dixon's Line, his haunting music evokes the joys and sorrows of plantation life in the days before the Civil War. Foster's best-known songs include "Old Folks at Home," "Oh, Susannah," and "I Dream of Jeanie with the Light Brown Hair." His songs were immensely popular during his lifetime, but alcoholism and a poor business sense drove Foster into poverty. He died in a New York charity hospital in 1864, with only thirty-eight cents in his pocket.

Another Pennsylvanian to achieve worldwide acclaim was contralto singer Marian Anderson. Born in 1902 to a poor black family in Philadelphia, Anderson joined the choir at the Union Baptist Church when she was eight years old. The congregation recognized her talent and raised money for her education. She spent several years in Europe, studying voice and giving concerts. Despite her ability, she fought many battles against racial discrimination in the United States. In 1955, Marian Anderson became the first black singer ever to perform at the Metropolitan Opera House in New York. The great conductor Arturo Toscanini said Anderson had "a voice found once in a century."

Pennsylvanians have a high regard for classical music. For three days each May, thousands of music lovers flock to Bethlehem for the annual Bach Festival, held on the campus of Lehigh University. The Pittsburgh Symphony, under the baton of Lorin Maazel, is one of the nation's leading orchestras. The symphony dazzles audiences at the Heinz Hall for the Performing Arts, a splendidly restored nineteenth-century theater.

Founded in 1900, the Philadelphia Orchestra has known such outstanding conductors as Leopold Stokowski and Eugene Ormandy. Since 1980 it has been conducted by Riccardo Muti. The orchestra performs at the Philadelphia Academy of Music, considered one of the most acoustically perfect concert halls in the

Eugene Ormandy (inset) and Leopold Stokowski are among the outstanding musicians who have conducted the Philadelphia Orchestra. Now under the direction of Riccardo Muti, the orchestra performs at the Academy of Music, one of the most acoustically perfect concert halls in the world (above).

world. Designed by Napoleon Le Brun and constructed in 1857, the building was allowed to stand roofless for a year to let the timbers age naturally for the best possible resonance. Next door to the concert hall stands the Curtis Institute of Music, one of the country's finest conservatories.

SPORTS

Football is an important college sport in Pennsylvania. Penn State University under coach Joe Paterno—acclaimed as Coach of the Year in 1978 and 1986—has fielded powerhouse teams for many years. The school's arch rival is the University of Pittsburgh. The annual Pitt vs. Penn State games are a civil war. In the 1970s,

Pennsylvania sports fans are proud of the fact that 76ers star Julius ''Dr. J.'' Erving (above) is recognized as one of the most exciting basketball players who ever played the game; that the Eagles (who play at Veterans Stadium, top right) went to the Super Bowl in 1981; and that the steel town of Aliquippa (right) has produced many outstanding athletes.

dazzling halfback Tony Dorsett, who grew up in the steel town of Aliquippa, starred for Pitt. Other outstanding football players from the state's harsh coal and mill towns include celebrated quarterback Joe Namath and Chicago Bears coach Mike Ditka.

Professional baseball teams are the Pittsburgh Pirates and the Philadelphia Phillies. Over their long histories, both of these National League organizations have produced championship teams and great individual players. Sharp-hitting Paul Waner starred with the Pirates in the 1920s and 1930s. Pittsburgh's

Roberto Clemente played with a rare blend of fire and talent. Clemente was killed in a 1972 airplane crash while delivering medical supplies to earthquake victims in Nicaragua. For many years, Willie Stargell was a fan favorite in Pittsburgh. Stargell was elected to the Baseball Hall of Fame in 1988, his first year of eligibility. Fans in Philadelphia cheered when players such as Mike Schmidt and Steve Carlton gave the city a powerful team in the 1970s and 1980s.

The Pittsburgh Steelers of the 1970s were one of the greatest pro football teams ever assembled. Led by strong-armed quarterback Terry Bradshaw, fleet and graceful wide receiver Lynn Swann, and rugged defensive lineman "Mean" Joe Green, the team won Super Bowls in 1975 and 1976 and again in 1979 and 1980. The year 1979 was especially joyous in Pittsburgh because the baseball Pirates and the football Steelers both won world championships. In Philadelphia the pro football Eagles have had far less success than their cross-state rivals. However, the Eagles fielded a strong team in the late 1970s and went to the Super Bowl in 1981. Hockey's Philadelphia Flyers were an outstanding team in the 1970s when led by star skater Bobby Clarke.

For many years the Philadelphia 76ers have been a mighty pro basketball team. At one time, the entire National Basketball Association (NBA) focused on the competition between the 76ers and the Boston Celtics. Towering Wilt Chamberlain and sharp-shooting Billy Cunningham were stellar performers for Philadelphia. Julius "Dr. J" Erving was a 76er star hailed as one of the most exciting men who ever played the game. "The Doctor"—so nicknamed because of the way he "operated" on the court—seemed to defy gravity as he soared above the floor, taking the ball to the hoop. Erving retired in 1987, with plans to turn his astonishing energy and talent to the field of business.

Chapter 10

A BRIEF TOUR OF THE KEYSTONE STATE

A BRIEF TOUR OF THE KEYSTONE STATE

From the shore of Lake Erie to the rugged Alleghenies, from small towns to bustling modern cities, a trip through Pennsylvania is study in contrasts. Gold-lettered historical markers stand along the highways, reminders of Pennsylvania's colorful past. Festivals, art museums, and quiet country walks are only a few of the attractions of the Keystone State.

THE ERIE TRIANGLE

The region known as the Erie Triangle is the only portion of Pennsylvania that was not included in William Penn's original land grant. Eager for access to the Great Lakes, in 1788 the state purchased territory that included forty miles (sixty-four kilometers) of lakefront from the federal government. Erie, the third-largest city in Pennsylvania, stands on the site of Fort Presque, built by the French in 1753.

Erie's shipyards contributed many frigates to the American fleet when the United States fought Great Britain in the War of 1812. Among them was the *Niagara*, which turned the tide in the Battle of Lake Erie. From its deck, Captain Oliver Hazard Perry sent his famous message, "We have met the enemy, and they are ours."

Geographically, the flat, low-lying plain around Erie has little in common with the rest of Pennsylvania. The people of the region,

Visitors to Presque Isle State Park, in the Erie Triangle, enjoy such activities as fishing (left), hiking, boating, and swimming. Oliver Hazard Perry's flagship *Niagara* (above) is displayed in a lakefront park in Erie.

too, feel closer to Buffalo, Detroit, and other Great Lake ports than they do to other Pennsylvania cities. With its vineyards and wineries, with its 3,200-acre (1,295-hectare) Presque Isle Wildlife Refuge, with fishing for muskellunge and coho salmon along the lake shore, the Erie Triangle is rich with surprises.

THE WESTERN HILLS

South and east of Erie, the vast Allegheny National Forest sprawls over 500,000 acres (202,343 hectares), a delight to lovers of the outdoors. Other parklands in northwestern Pennsylvania include the Cook Forest, the Tionesta Scenic Area, and Heart's Content State Park.

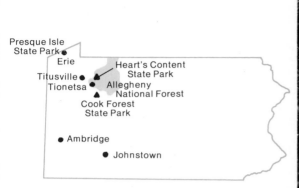

A replica of Edwin L. Drake's oil well near Titusville marks the site of America's first commercial oil well.

At the Drake's Well Museum near Titusville in Venango County, full-sized replicas of Edwin L. Drake's original shed and derrick mark the site of America's first commercial oil well. The oil rush of the 1860s left Venango County peppered with ghost towns, forlorn reminders of the saga of "boom and bust." When drillers struck oil at Pit Hole City in 1865, fifteen thousand people flocked to the town, dreaming of fortunes to be made. But within a year the wells began to run dry. By 1867, weeds choked the once-busy streets, and Pit Hole City stood abandoned. Today a small museum displays dioramas of early drilling operations and a scale model of the town in its days of glory.

Pennsylvania's most extensive deposits of bituminous coal lie in the western half of the state. The most efficient method of extracting it from the ground is strip mining, tearing away sheets of earth to reach the coal beneath. In Pennsylvania, strict laws help to minimize the damage strip mining causes to the landscape. Scores of resorts have been created in this area, known to visitors as the Laurel Highlands.

The top portion of this inclined plane railway overlooks the steel
town of Johnstown on the Conemaugh River, the site of an 1889 flood
that was one of the worst natural disasters in American history.

The city of Johnstown lies in the heart of soft-coal country, and
is a major steel-manufacturing center. But to many Americans, the
name still evokes the terrible flood of 1889. On May 31, the South
Fork Dam on the Conemaugh River burst after heavy rains, and a
great wall of water roared downstream to engulf the city. Some
twenty-two hundred men, women, and children died in the
Johnstown Flood, one of the worst natural disasters in American
history. Rows of black headstones in the Grandview Cemetery
mark the graves of hundreds of flood victims whose bodies were
never identified.

Near the town of Ambridge in Beaver County, eighteen restored
homes and factory buildings recreate life in the village of
Economy. Founded in 1825 by a German religious sect called the
Harmony Society, Economy became a thriving textile center.
Members donated all of their worldly goods to the community
and wove beautiful woolen, cotton, and silk fabrics while they
awaited the second coming of Christ.

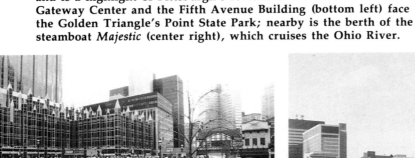

Pittsburgh

The **Pittsburgh Plate Glass Building** (bottom right and detail, top right) forms a glittering background for **Market Square** (top left) and is a highlight of Pittsburgh's revitalized downtown district. **Gateway Center** and the **Fifth Avenue Building** (bottom left) face the **Golden Triangle's Point State Park;** nearby is the berth of the steamboat *Majestic* (center right), which cruises the **Ohio River.**

THE NATION'S MOST LIVABLE CITY

In 1946, Pittsburgh's Mayor David Lawrence described his city as the "dirtiest slag pile in the United States." Since World War II, however, Pittsburgh has seen dramatic changes. Steel plants and other factories poured millions of dollars into smoke-abatement programs. Civic leaders worked to improve the city's schools, highways, and social services. The Gateway Center, a striking complex of brightly colored skyscrapers, revitalized the "Golden Triangle," Pittsburgh's downtown business district.

At the tip of the Golden Triangle, where the Allegheny and Monongahela rivers join to form the Ohio, lies the 36-acre (14.6-hectare) Point State Park. Within the park stands Fort Pitt's original brick blockhouse, built in 1764. The Fort Pitt Museum displays weapons, uniforms, and other memorabilia of the city's early days as a military outpost on the frontier.

The park offers an excellent view of the rivers that have played such a central role in Pittsburgh's history. Pittsburgh remains a major inland port, with great tugboats plying their way upstream and downstream. A replica of a nineteenth-century steamboat cruises the Ohio between Pittsburgh and Emsworth, offering passengers a glimpse of the romantic early days on the river.

Despite the industry's decline, steel plants in and around Pittsburgh still employ thousands of workers. Pittsburgh is also home to many of America's leading corporations, including USX Corporation, formerly called U.S. Steel; Alcoa Aluminum; and Rockwell International. The main offices of the Pittsburgh Plate Glass Company are housed in a spectacular forty-story building forming a tower of mirrors.

Pittsburgh is also a seat of culture and learning. The Carnegie includes the Library of Pittsburgh, the Museum of Art, the

Among the many legacies of philanthropists Andrew Carnegie and Andrew Mellon are Pittsburgh's Carnegie Mellon University (above), dedicated to industrial research, and the Carnegie Museum of Art (right).

Museum of National History, the Buhl Science Center, and the Music Hall. The Frick Art Museum has an outstanding permanent collection. The University of Pittsburgh encompasses seventeen liberal-arts and professional schools. Carnegie-Mellon University is dedicated to industrial research.

In 1985, many Americans were amazed when the Rand McNally *Places Rated Almanac* called Pittsburgh the "most livable city in the nation." But the people of Pittsburgh, proud of their city's accomplishments, were not at all surprised.

CENTRAL PENNSYLVANIA

Few small towns in the world attract more visitors than Gettysburg. More than fourteen hundred monuments, statues, and markers in the extensive Gettysburg National Military Park

The thousands of graves in Gettysburg National Cemetery (above) and hundreds of monuments, statues, markers, and weapons (right) in Gettysburg National Military Park are reminders of the bloodiest battle ever fought in North America.

commemorate the bloodiest battle ever fought in North America. Visitors can retrace the movements of the troops at such landmarks as McPherson Ridge, Cemetery Hill, Little Round Top, and Devil's Bend. The Gettysburg National Cemetery, which Lincoln dedicated with his famous address, is the final resting place of thousands of Union soldiers from the Civil War, as well as veterans of all of the wars in which the United States has fought since that time.

Another Gettysburg landmark is the home of President Dwight D. Eisenhower. In 1950, two years before he became president of the United States, Eisenhower purchased an eighteenth-century farmhouse that he described as "an escape from concrete into the countryside." In 1955, when Eisenhower was recovering from a near-fatal heart attack, his Gettysburg retreat became the temporary White House.

At the annual Kutztown Pennsylvania Dutch Folk Festival, visitors may buy handmade quilts, dolls, and even straw mobiles (above), and sample such delicacies as scrapple, apple snitz, and molasses pie.

One of the most popular attractions for visitors to Pennsylvania is the "Pennsylvania Dutch country" of Berks, York, and Lancaster counties. Some barns are still painted with brightly colored geometric "hex signs," which German settlers once believed would keep away witches. Amish farmers work their fields with horse-drawn plows and drive their families to town in black buggies. At the annual Pennsylvania Dutch Folk Festival, held in Kutztown each June, visitors may buy handmade quilts and dolls, and sample such delicacies as scrapple, apple snitz (fried apple strips), and molasses pie. At the Farmers Market in downtown Lancaster, Amish families sell the fruits and vegetables they have harvested from their own land.

Lancaster is also the site of Wheatland, the fully restored home of James Buchanan. Born in Mercersburg, Buchanan served as fifteenth president of the United States. He is the only native Pennsylvanian ever to hold that office.

Two of central Pennsylvania's unusual attractions are the nation's oldest pretzel factory, in Lititz (far left), and the chocolate town of Hershey, with streetlamps shaped like candy kisses and a lovely rock garden (left).

Just north of Lancaster, the nation's oldest pretzel factory operates in Lititz. Some pretzels are cooked in ovens that date back to the bakery's founding. Tours include a hands-on demonstration of how to shape and roll the dough. Visitors must buy one pretzel as a ticket of admission.

The aroma of chocolate drifts over the city of Hershey, where the streetlamps are shaped like candy kisses. There are daily tours of the factory that has turned out candy bars and cocoa since 1903—a chocolate lover's paradise.

On the east bank of the Susquehanna stands Harrisburg, Pennsylvania's capital since 1812. Completed in 1906, the State Capitol has been called the finest in the nation. The main building is crowned by an immense green dome, modeled after the dome of St. Peter's Cathedral in Rome. A long series of broad steps leads to the triple arches of the entrance. Inside, the senate chamber is adorned with murals depicting the formation and preservation of the Union.

The State Museum at Harrisburg is housed in the William Penn Memorial Building, which contains Penn's original charter to Pennsylvania. The museum has exhibits on the state's natural history, Indian cultures, and transportation, as well as Pennsylvania German crafts.

Williamsport, once the lumber capital of the world, is now the home of the Little League Hall of Fame and the site of the Little League World Series.

Eighty miles (129 kilometers) to the north, up the Susquehanna, is Williamsport. From 1855 until the 1880s, Williamsport was the lumber capital of the world. Lumbermen steered giant rafts of logs to Williamsport's mills, where they were sawed into boards. Today Williamsport hosts the Little League Baseball World Series each August, and fans can examine the memorabilia in the Little League Hall of Fame.

THE EASTERN CITIES

In the Wyoming Valley of northeastern Pennsylvania, the cities of Scranton and Wilkes-Barre lie in the heart of hard-coal country. During the late 1700s, Connecticut claimed the Wyoming Valley as part of its own territory. In 1800, after a series of skirmishes called the Yankee Pennamite Wars, the dispute was settled in Pennsylvania's favor.

Hard-coal production has tapered off in recent decades, but tours of a reconstructed mine at the Anthracite Museum in Ashland provide a glimpse of the miner's trade. The museum is adjacent to the Lackawanna Mine Tour, an underground visitor's excursion. At Eckley Miner's Village, a nineteenth-century mining town has been restored in fascinating detail.

The Pocono region in the northeast corner of the state is sometimes called "Pennsylvania's playground." In the winter, skiers sweep down the mountainsides, and skaters glide over the frozen lakes. Whizzing down the 1,200-foot (366-meter) slide at Eaglesmere Lake, toboggans may reach a speed of forty-five miles per hour (seventy-two kilometers per hour). During the warmer months, Lake Wallenpaupack, Lake Silkworth, Harvey's Lake, and nearly two hundred others offer swimming, sailing, waterskiing, and fishing. The stunning scenery at the Delaware Water Gap, where the river rushes through a gorge below the mountain crest, has inspired artists since the 1820s.

Straddling the Lehigh River are the industrial cities of Allentown and Bethlehem. The Liberty Bell Shrine at Allentown's Zion United Church of Christ commemorates the months when the Liberty Bell was hidden here during the revolutionary war. A replica of the bell stands where the actual Liberty Bell was once concealed beneath the church's floorboards.

Steel capital of eastern Pennsylvania, Bethlehem was founded by Moravian Count Zinzendorf in 1741. Arriving on Christmas Eve, the count and his followers shared a two-room log cabin with a group of cows. Remembering the story of Christ in the manger, they named their new town Bethlehem. Today, Bethlehem's choir sings an annual Christmas concert that is famous throughout the world.

Farther to the south, on the Schuylkill River, lies Valley Forge

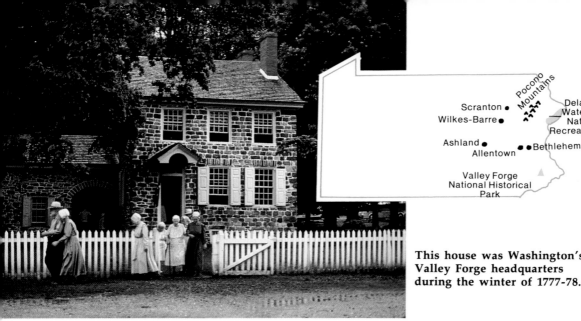

This house was Washington's Valley Forge headquarters during the winter of 1777-78.

National Historical Park. Visitors can see Washington's headquarters and several restored huts where troops lived during the encampment of winter 1777-78. To the south, Washington Crossing State Park marks the spot where the general crossed the Delaware with twenty-four hundred men to capture Trenton, New Jersey.

THE CITY OF BROTHERLY LOVE

"Yes—Philadelphia. I wanted to go there once but it was closed," comic W. C. Fields once quipped. Despite the vaudeville jokes, Philadelphia is an exciting city—modern, yet steeped in three centuries of history.

With thirty-six brick houses just as they were two hundred years ago, Elfreth's Alley is the oldest unchanged street in the United States. On the first Saturday in June each year, the people of Elfreth's Alley dress in colonial costumes and open these early houses to the public.

Memories of the revolutionary war abound in Philadelphia. There is Carpenters' Hall, where the First Continental Congress met in 1774. A wide, grassy mall leads to the State House, now

The First Continental Congress met at Carpenters' Hall in Philadelphia.

Independence Hall, where Congress met during most of the revolutionary war. Independence Hall served as the seat of government under the Articles of Confederation, and the Constitutional Convention met there during the summer of 1787.

The Liberty Bell, which rang out news of independence from the tower of the State House on July 8, 1776, is now housed in a pavilion of its own a few blocks away. Cast in London in 1751, the bell is engraved with the Biblical quotation, "Proclaim liberty throughout all the land, unto all the inhabitants thereof." The bell cracked in 1835 and has never rung again.

It would be impossible to visit all of the one hundred or more museums in the Philadelphia area. One of the most interesting is the Franklin Institute of Science, where visitors walk through a two-story model of the human heart. On the same grounds, Fell's Planetarium presents spellbinding views of the heavens. The Academy of Natural Science is the oldest natural history museum in the United States.

Rooms at the Philadelphia Museum of Art recreate a Japanese

teahouse, a Hindu shrine, and an eighteenth-century Dutch parlor in precise detail. The adjoining Rodin Museum contains the most complete collection of sculpture outside of Paris by the French Impressionist master. Another fine art museum is the Pennsylvania Academy of the Fine Arts, designed in 1876 by noted Philadelphia architect Frank Furness.

Philadelphia is still a city of parks, as William Penn intended when he designed his "country town." Fairmount Park, covering 8,000 acres (3,237 hectares) and stretching 10 miles (16 kilometers) from the northwest city limits to City Hall, is the largest landscaped city park in the world. The Philadelphia Orchestra gives outdoor concerts each summer at the park's Mann Music Center. The John B. Kelly Playhouse, the Philadelphia Zoo, and a variety of furnished historic houses are all located within the park.

For generations, an unwritten rule in Philadelphia forbade any building to reach higher than the crown of William Penn's hat— that is, the top of the statue on the forty-story City Hall. But in December 1985, Mayor Wilson Goode inaugurated One Liberty Place, a striking new skyscraper designed by Helmut Jahn that rises sixty-one stories high. "This building breaks the status quo in the city," Goode declared. "It says we have arrived." Philadelphia is a city that cherishes its traditions, but never lets custom stand in the way of progress.

The immortal words of William Penn encircle the great dome of the Capitol in Harrisburg: "This hope is for the state: that there may be room there for a holy experiment, and my God will make it the seed of a nation." As a pioneer of industry and a cultural leader in the nation's development, Pennsylvania has fulfilled its founder's dearest hopes.

Philadelphia, home of such historic shrines as the Liberty Bell (above), is also a city of parks, people, and famous buildings. Fairmount Park (bottom left) is the world's largest landscaped city park; Eakins Square (left) is a popular gathering place; and City Hall (below) marks the end of beautiful Benjamin Franklin Parkway.

FACTS AT A GLANCE

GENERAL INFORMATION

Statehood: December 12, 1787, second state

Origin of Name: The official name is Commonwealth of Pennsylvania. At the time the name was adopted, the words *state* and *commonwealth* were considered to be synonymous. The name Pennsylvania, meaning "Penn's Woods," was given to the land by King Charles II of England in honor of Admiral William Penn, father of Pennsylvania's founder.

State Capital: Harrisburg

State Nickname: "Keystone State"; also called "Quaker State"

State Flag: The state flag was adopted in 1907. Centered on a blue field, two black horses support the state coat of arms, which displays a sailing ship, a plow, and three sheaves of wheat, representing commerce and agriculture; an eagle, which stands for speed, strength, bravery, and wisdom; a cornstalk, which symbolizes prosperity; and an olive branch, which represents peace. Below the coat of arms is the state motto.

State Motto: "Virtue, Liberty, and Independence"

State Bird: Ruffed grouse

State Animal: White-tailed deer

State Dog: Great Dane

State Insect: Firefly

State Fish: Brook trout

State Flower: Mountain laurel

State Tree: Eastern hemlock

State Song: None

POPULATION

Population: 11,881,643, fifth among the states (1990 census)

Population Density: 262 people per sq.mi. (101 people per km²)

Population Distribution: 69 percent of the people live in cities or towns. Philadelphia, Pennsylvania's largest city, ranks fourth in population size in the nation. Nearly 50 percent of the people live in or near Philadelphia and Pittsburgh.

Philadelphia	1,585,577
Pittsburgh	369,879
Erie	108,718
Allentown	105,090
Scranton	81,805
Reading	78,380
Bethlehem	71,428
Lancaster	55,551
Harrisburg	52,376

(Population figures according to 1990 census)

Population Growth: Pennsylvania's population increased steadily from colonial times through the years before the Civil War. Industrialization in the late nineteenth and early twentieth centuries brought tens of thousands of immigrants into the state from Europe. After the 1950s, population growth slowed. In the decade from 1980 to 1990, Pennsylvania's population grew less than 1 percent, compared to the national growth rate of 9.8 percent. The list below shows population growth in Pennsylvania since 1820:

Year	Population
1820	1,049,458
1840	1,724,033
1860	2,906,215
1880	4,282,591
1900	6,302,115
1920	8,720,017
1940	9,900,180
1950	10,498,012
1960	11,319,366
1970	11,793,909
1980	11,864,751
1990	11,881,643

GEOGRAPHY

Borders: States that border Pennsylvania are New York on the north, New York and New Jersey on the east (separated from Pennsylvania by the Delaware River), Delaware on the southeast, Maryland and West Virginia on the south, and West Virginia and Ohio on the west. Lake Erie forms the state's northwest boundary.

A waterfall in scenic upstate Pennsylvania

Highest Point: Mount Davis, 3,213 ft. (979 m), in Somerset County

Lowest Point: Sea level, along the Delaware River

Greatest Distances: North to south—169 mi. (272 km)
East to west—307 mi. (494 km)

Area: 45,302 sq.mi. (117,332 km²)

Rank in Area Among the States: Thirty-third

Rivers: Nearly forty-five hundred rivers and streams crisscross Pennsylvania. Three major river systems provide 95 percent of the drainage in the state: the Ohio, the Susquehanna, and the Delaware. The Ohio River system drains most of western Pennsylvania and is a major transportation route in the state. From Pittsburgh, where the Allegheny and the Monongahela join to form the Ohio, the river flows, via the Mississippi, to empty into the Gulf of Mexico. Pennsylvania's Beaver, Clarion, and Youghiogheny rivers also are important parts of the Ohio River system. Central Pennsylvania, almost 50 percent of the total state area, is drained by the wide but shallow Susquehanna, which originates in New York state. Its main tributaries are the West Branch and the Juniata. The Susquehanna is only partly navigable. It meanders through the state, eventually entering the Atlantic Ocean via Maryland and Chesapeake Bay. The Delaware River and its main tributaries, the Lehigh and Schuylkill, drain eastern Pennsylvania. The Delaware forms Pennsylvania's eastern border. It empties into the Atlantic Ocean via Delaware Bay and is navigable by oceangoing ships. Majestic Delaware Gap, other deep-cut gorges, and spectacular waterfalls in the Pocono Mountains contribute to eastern Pennsylvania's reputation as a scenic and recreational wonderland.

The fertile farmlands of Lancaster County are in the Piedmont region.

Lakes: Pennsylvania has more than three hundred natural and artificial lakes. Lake Conneaut is the largest natural lake lying totally within state boundaries. Other scenic natural lakes dot the state's northeast and northwest. Lake Wallenpaupack, in the Poconos, is the largest man-made lake lying totally within the state. Pennsylvania's largest lake by far, the Pymatuning Reservoir on the Pennsylvania-Ohio border, is shared by the two states. In the northwest, Pennsylvania has 40 mi. (64 km) of waterfront along Lake Erie, giving the state access to Great Lakes shipping.

Topography: Tens of millions of years ago, a lofty mountain chain as high as the Swiss Alps ran through what is now the Piedmont in eastern Pennsylvania. West of the mountains was a vast bay. Then came a series of disruptions: volcanic action, erosion, the heaving and buckling of mountain formation, and, in the Ice Age, a glacier nearly .5 mi. (.8 km) thick in northern Pennsylvania. Over a period of 400 million years, the bay waters drained, leaving behind a worn-down Piedmont and, to the west, a vast bed of coal in the Allegheny Mountains and Plateau. Today, Pennsylvania spreads across seven topographical regions: the Atlantic Coastal Plain, the Piedmont, the New England Upland, the Blue Ridge, the Appalachian Ridge and Valley Region, the Appalachian Plateau, and the Erie Lowland.

In southeastern Pennsylvania, the Atlantic Coastal Plain occupies the extreme southeastern tip of the state. It is a low, level area, reaching sea level along the Delaware River. The Philadelphia metropolitan area covers most of the region. North and west of Philadelphia lies the Piedmont, a belt of land extending inland

60 to 100 mi. (96 to 161 km), with altitudes rising to 800 ft. (244 m). The fertile Pennsylvania Dutch farmlands of Lancaster and York counties are in the Piedmont region. North of the Piedmont, the New England Upland is a narrow ridge across Berks, Bucks, Lehigh, and Northampton counties. West of the Piedmont, in south-central Pennsylvania, a northern finger of the Blue Ridge juts up into the state. Locally known as South Mountain, this was the site of the Battle of Gettysburg. Curving north and west of the Piedmont is the Appalachian Ridge and Valley Region, a series of parallel ridges and valleys cut by the Susquehanna River. The region's principal valley, the Great Valley, extends from the east-central to the south-central border of the state and is divided into the Lehigh, Cumberland, and Lebanon valleys. The valleys contain fertile farmland; the eastern part of the ridges contain world-famous Pennsylvania anthracite (hard coal).

The Appalachian Plateau, known in Pennsylvania as the Allegheny Plateau, covers most of northern and western Pennsylvania and occupies almost one half of its total land area. Rugged and heavily forested, the Appalachian Plateau consists of deep, narrow valleys and high, broad ridges. The Pocono Mountains rise more than 2,000 ft. (610 m) at the eastern end of the Appalachian Plateau; Mount Davis, the state's highest point at 3,213 ft. (979 m), rises in the Allegheny Mountains in the southeast. The region along the eastern edge of the Appalachian Plateau where it meets the Allegheny Ridge and Valley Region is called the Allegheny Front. The western Appalachian Plateau is mined for bituminous (soft) coal, gas, and oil. In the extreme northwest corner of the state, the Appalachian Plateau slopes down to the Erie Lowland, a narrow, flat region bordering Lake Erie. The northwestern lowland, around the city of Erie, is noted for its production of grapes, other fruits, and vegetables.

Climate: Pennsylvania's climate is temperate, with warm, humid summers and cold winters. Temperatures vary across the state depending on the season, region, and altitude. The southern and eastern regions tend to be warmer than the northern and western ones. Philadelphia, in the southeast, has an average July temperature of 77° F. (25° C) and an average January temperature of 34° F. (1.1° C). Pittsburgh, in the southeast, averages 75° F. (23.9° C) in July and 28° F. (-2.2° C) in January. The highest temperature ever recorded in the state was 111° F. (43.9° C) at Phoenixville on July 9 and 10, 1936. The lowest recorded temperature was -42° F. (-41.1° C) at Smethport in McKean County on January 5, 1904. Annual rainfall averages 42 in. (107 cm) across the state, with 34 to 44 in. (86 to 112 cm) in the northwest and 42 to 47 in. (107 to 119 cm) in the southeast. Annual snowfall ranges from an average of 20 in. (51 cm) at Philadelphia, to 45 in. (114 cm) at Pittsburgh, to more than 90 in. (229 cm) at Erie, in the snowbelt region. Both floods and hurricanes have caused severe damage in the state, notably the Johnstown Flood of 1889 and Hurricane Agnes in 1972.

NATURE

Trees: Ash, aspen, beech, birch, cherry, chestnut, elm, hackberry, hemlock, hickory, linden, locust, maple, oak, pine, poplar, sycamore, tulip, black walnut, and willow

Wild Plants: Azalea, black-eyed Susan, wild columbine, dewberry, dogwood, fern, wild ginger, hawthorn, honeysuckle, Juneberry, mountain laurel, rhododendron, violet, and wintergreen

Animals: Bear, deer, fox, ground hog, opossum, mink, muskrat, rabbit, raccoon, skunk, squirrel, weasel, and wildcat

Birds: Blue jay, cardinal, wood dove, duck, flicker, ruffed grouse, killdeer, pheasant, quail, robin, tufted titmouse, sparrow, barn swallow, vireo, and cedar waxwing

Fish: Pennsylvania has more than 150 species of fish, including bass, carp, catfish, chub, perch, pickerel, pike, and trout; reptiles include frogs, toads, and lizards.

GOVERNMENT

The government of Pennsylvania, like that of the federal government, is divided into three branches: executive, legislative, and judicial. The state's legislative branch, the General Assembly, is made up of a 203-member house of representatives and a 50-member senate. Senators are elected to four-year terms and representatives to two-year terms. Regular sessions of the legislature are held on even-numbered years and last from January to November.

The executive branch, headed by the governor, administers the law. The governor is elected to a four-year term, and may not serve more than two consecutive terms. The governor appoints the secretary of state, adjutant general, and several other high officers. The lieutenant governor, attorney general, state treasurer, and auditor general are elected directly by the people to four-year terms. The governor may veto legislation, call special sessions of the legislature, and propose the state budget.

The judicial branch interprets laws and tries cases. The supreme court is the highest tribunal in the state. Its seven judges are elected to seven-year terms. Pennsylvania's superior court has fifteen judges, five of whom are senior judges. Judges of the superior court hold sessions each year in Harrisburg, Philadelphia, Pittsburgh, and Scranton. Pennsylvania also has a commonwealth court with nine judges. Superior and commonwealth-court judges are elected to ten-year terms and may be reelected. All Pennsylvania judges must retire by the age of seventy, except for the senior judges of the superior court, who have no mandatory retirement age.

Number of Counties: 67

U.S. Representatives: 23

Electoral Votes: 25

Voting Qualifications: United States citizen, eighteen years of age, at least a thirty-day residency in Pennsylvania and the voting district

EDUCATION

Public education in Pennsylvania is under the control of the Department of Education. The state spends about $5.5 billion on public education each year. About 840,000 Pennsylvania students are enrolled in public elementary schools, and an equal number are enrolled in public secondary schools. Another 370,000 students, or 18 percent of the total, are enrolled in private elementary and secondary schools.

Pennsylvania has more than two hundred institutions of higher learning, with an enrollment of more than 500,000 students. An additional 90,000 or so attend community colleges. Universities that receive state aid include Pennsylvania State University at University Park, Temple University in Philadelphia, and the University of Pittsburgh. Private colleges and universities include Bryn Mawr; Haverford; Swarthmore; Villanova; the University of Pennsylvania, Drexel, La Salle, and St. Joseph's, all in Philadelphia; Carnegie-Mellon University and Duquesne University in Pittsburgh; Bucknell University in Lewisburg; Dickinson University in Carlisle; Franklin and Marshall in Lancaster; Lehigh and Moravian in Bethlehem; Lafayette in Easton; Muhlenberg in Allentown; and Gettysburg.

ECONOMY AND INDUSTRY

Principal Products:
Agriculture: Cattle, hogs, sheep, dairy products, poultry, eggs, turkeys, wool, corn, hay, wheat, soybeans, rye, oats, barley, tobacco, potatoes, tomatoes, beans, apples, peaches, grapes, strawberries, cherries, pears, mushrooms, greenhouse and nursery products
Manufacturing: Cement, primary metals, nonelectrical machinery, fabricated metals, transportation equipment, petroleum refining, electrical machinery, pharmaceuticals
Natural Resources: Bituminous (soft) and anthracite (hard) coal, petroleum, iron, limestone, clay, sand, gravel, natural gas

Business and Trade: Philadelphia, with its busy international port, is one of the nation's leading trade centers and home to the nation's fifth-largest stock exchange. Retail trade has been important in Pennsylvania since the 1870s, when John Wanamaker opened the nation's first department store and Frank Woolworth developed a successful five-and-dime store in the state. The Kresge, Murphy, Newberry, and W. T. Grant chains also were founded in Pennsylvania. Today some 66 percent of the state's gross product (annual total value of goods and services produced) comes from the fast-growing service industries—retail and wholesale trade, and business, social, and personal services. Almost half of Pennsylvania's workers are employed in the service industries. Although manufacturing, once the backbone of the state's economy, employs about one fourth of Pennsylvania's work force, workers in the health-care services alone now outnumber those engaged in the manufacture of metals. Philadelphia is becoming a center for high-tech industries (computer, computer-related, and electronic industries), with nearly 100 firms employing 80,000 people. Pittsburgh has become a center for corporate headquarters, the third-largest in the nation. Pennsylvania's historic, cultural, and recreational facilities have long made the state a favorite tourist spot. Tourism brings some $8 billion into the state each year and generates almost 200,000 jobs.

Finance: Philadelphia is Pennsylvania's center for banking and insurance. The state has nearly 200 national banks, with assets in excess of $60 billion, and another 150 state-chartered banks with assets of more than $50 billion. In addition, there are more than 250 state and federal savings-and-loan associations with assets of $25 billion. More than 1,300 insurance companies operate in the state. Of these, 341 are Pennsylvania-based.

Communication: Pennsylvania has approximately 100 daily newspapers and about 175 weeklies. The *Philadelphia Inquirer*, the *Pittsburgh Post-Gazette*, the *Allentown Morning Call*, and the *Bethlehem Globe-Times* are among the state's largest daily newspapers. Small daily newspapers of note include the *Pottsville Republican*, the *Tarentum Valley News Dispatch*, the *Beaver County Times*, and a Hatboro paper called *Today's Spirit*. KDKA in Pittsburgh was the nation's first commercial radio station. It began broadcasting on November 2, 1920. Pennsylvania has about 360 radio stations and 35 television stations.

Transportation: There are about 700 airports in Pennsylvania. Its more than 160 commercial airports include the Greater Pittsburgh Airport, the state's busiest, and the Philadelphia International Airport, the state's second busiest.
   Seven passenger railroads serving nearly thirty cities cross the state. The nearly fifty freight companies that operate in Pennsylvania carry one sixth of the nation's total rail tonnage each year on approximately 9,000 mi. (14,484 km) of track.
   Pennsylvania has approximately 28,000 mi. (45,062 km) of urban highways and 90,000 mi. (144,841 km) of rural highways. The Pennsylvania Turnpike, opened in 1940, was the nation's first major limited-access highway; nearly 70 million passenger vehicles and 12 million commercial vehicles use it each year. Other major roads in Pennsylvania include Interstate 80, which crosses the state from east to west; Interstate 81, which goes north to south via Scranton, Wilkes-Barre, and Harrisburg; and Interstate 79, which traverses the state north to south, from Erie to the West Virginia border via Pittsburgh.
   Philadelphia, Pittsburgh, and Erie are the state's major shipping ports. Metropolitan Philadelphia is the second-largest seaport on the Atlantic coast, and the fifth-largest in the United States. Nearly 64 million short tons (59 million metric tons) of cargo a year are handled at the ports of Philadelphia, 31 percent of the total tonnage handled at all North Atlantic coast ports.

SOCIAL AND CULTURAL LIFE

Museums: Philadelphia has many fine museums. Among the most prominent are the Philadelphia Museum of Art, which is noted for its superb Italian Renaissance collection; the Rodin Museum, which has one of the world's best and largest indoor and outdoor collections of sculptures by Rodin; the Pennsylvania

Academy of the Fine Arts; the Art Alliance; and the Barnes Museum. The Franklin Institute contains a science museum and a planetarium. Chinese sculpture, Babylonian art, and Middle American, Pacific, and African art are on exhibit at the Museum of the University of Pennsylvania. The Philadelphia Zoo, the state's largest, is located in Fairmount Park.

In Pittsburgh, the Carnegie Museum of Art and the Frick Museum of Art are outstanding for their collections of classic and modern works. Pennsylvania's artistic, cultural, and natural-history heritages are richly displayed at the State Museum in Harrisburg. The Pennsylvania Farm Museum near Lancaster interprets traditional Pennsylvania rural life with exhibits of folk art showing domestic and farm practices. The Somerset Historical Center recalls the fervent pioneering spirit of those who settled the Pennsylvania frontier. State and national military history are preserved at the Fort Pitt Museum in Pittsburgh, the Pennsylvania Military Museum in Boalsburg, and in displays at Valley Forge and Gettysburg. The Hessian Powder Museum at Carlisle displays the history of Carlisle Barracks and of the Carlisle Indian School made famous by football hero and Olympic athlete Jim Thorpe. Harrisburg's Museum of Scientific Discovery is a participatory museum where children and adults explore the wonders of the world. Specialized museums depicting Pennsylvania's industry include the Drake Well Museum in Titusville, site of the world's first oil well; the Pennsylvania Lumber Museum at Galeton; the Railroad Museum at Strasburg; the Canal Museum at Easton; Anthracite museums at Ashland and Scranton; and the Miners' Village at Eckley.

Libraries: There are more than 630 public libraries in the state. The Philadelphia Free Library, with more than 3 million volumes and 51 branches, is the state's largest. Pittsburgh, with 1.9 million volumes and 21 branches, has the state's second-largest public library system. Other large public library systems are those of Norristown, Erie, Allentown, Easton, Bethlehem, and Harrisburg. The State Library of Pennsylvania in Harrisburg has about 1 million volumes. The University of Pennsylvania Library is noted for its collections of medieval history, Shakespeare, Sanskrit, and Walt Whitman. Other large university libraries include those of the University of Pittsburgh, Penn State, Temple, Carnegie Mellon, and Swarthmore. The Alverthorpe Gallery Library in Jenkintown contains the Rosenwald collection of illustrated books that date back to the fifteenth century.

The Atheneum is a private library with an extensive collection on architecture. The Historical Society of Pennsylvania has one of the leading historical libraries in the country.

Performing Arts: The Philadelphia Orchestra has long been one of the nation's premier musical organizations. Under the leadership of Eugene Ormandy, and now Riccardo Muti, it has made more recordings of classical music than any other American orchestra. The Academy of Music, home of the Philadelphia Orchestra, is world famous for its fine acoustics. It is also the home of the Philly Pops, conducted by Peter Nero; the Opera Company of Philadelphia; and the Pennsylvania Ballet Company. Pennsylvania's other great orchestra, the Pittsburgh Symphony, performs at Heinz Hall for the Performing Arts, as do the Pittsburgh Ballet Theater, the Pittsburgh Opera Company, and the Civic Light Opera. Harrisburg boasts a symphony orchestra and two noted choral groups—the Chamber Singers and the Choral Society.

Philadelphia is a national center for the sport of rowing. In the spring and early summer, rowers congregate at this bathhouse on the Schuylkill River in Fairmount Park.

Sports and Recreation: Philadelphia is represented by teams in all of the major professional sports: the Eagles play in the National Football League (NFL); the Phillies play in baseball's National League (NL); the 76ers are a perennial contender in the National Basketball Association (NBA); and in ice hockey the city is represented by the Flyers, who play in the National Hockey League (NHL). Pittsburgh has the NFL Steelers; the NL Pirates; and the NHL Penguins. The Pocono International Raceway in Long Pond attracts world-class drivers and cars. Each year the Spectrum in Philadelphia is home to the National Indoor Tennis Championships. The Velodrome at Trexlertown, near Allentown, is home to some of America's top bicycle racing. Williamsport hosts the annual Little League World Series. For many years, Philadelphia has been a national center for the sport of rowing; between March and June, many highly ranked college athletes compete in regattas on the Schuylkill River.

Pennsylvania has one national forest, the Allegheny National Forest. The state's more than one hundred state parks offer both the natural beauty of the state and a taste of its history. Hiking, biking, skiing, snowmobiling, and water sports are very popular in the state. Pine Creek and the Youghiogheny and Lehigh rivers are outstanding for their white-water rapids and breathtaking scenery.

Bartram's Garden, the nation's oldest botanical garden, was established by Pennsylvanian John Bartram in 1728. Located in Philadelphia, its highlight is a historic plant collection. Fairmount Park, also in Philadelphia, is the largest landscaped park in the world. The park contains historic mansions, the Philadelphia Zoo, a horticultural center, and numerous formal gardens. The arboretum at Longwood Gardens in Kennett Square displays rare trees, shrubs, formal gardens, fountains and pools, and glass houses for orchids, ferns, and other special collections.

Historic Sites and Landmarks:

Daniel Boone Homestead, near Reading, is the birthplace of the frontiersman and national hero. The site includes the Boone home, a blacksmith shop, a barn, and a sawmill.

Brandywine Battlefield, at Chadds Ford, is the site of the 1777 revolutionary war battle in which Washington engaged the British for control of strategic territory near Philadelphia. There are exhibits and dioramas in the visitor center and there are two historic Quaker farmhouses on the site.

Cornwall Furnace, on Furnace Creek in Cornwall, is one of the few remaining examples of a colonial iron-smelting furnace. In operation from 1742 to 1883, Cornwall produced forty-two cannons for American patriots in the revolutionary war.

Eisenhower Farm, near Gettysburg, is now a National Historic Site. Here is where President Dwight D. Eisenhower and his wife Mamie retired in 1961 when his presidency ended.

Ephrata Cloister, between Lancaster and Reading, was a German Protestant religious community from 1732 until the early 1800s. The community was noted for the beautiful choral music written and sung there and for a steady production of printed books and religious tracts. Ten of the original buildings have been restored to recreate this unusual eighteenth-century communal village.

Flagship Niagara, docked at Erie, is a reconstruction of the square-rigged wooden warship from which Commander Oliver Hazard Perry defeated the British at the 1813 Battle of Lake Erie, during the War of 1812.

Fort Necessity, near Uniontown, is the reconstructed stockade where in 1754 General George Washington surrendered to the enemy during the French and Indian War. Fort Necessity National Battlefield, at nearby Jumonville Glen, marks the site of Washington's first military action in the war.

Gettysburg National Battlefield, at Gettysburg, was the site of the 1863 battle that marked the turning point in the Civil War. President Lincoln delivered his stirring Gettysburg Address here when he dedicated a National Cemetery at the site.

Hopewell Village, near Birdsboro, is a restored iron-making community that dates back to 1770. This National Historic Site presents a complete picture of life in an iron-making community of colonial America.

Old Economy Village, in Ambridge, was the final home of the Harmony Society, a religious community in existence from 1805 to 1905. The Harmonists, noted producers of shoes, textiles, and food crops, invested their income in local businesses and donated to charitable causes. Seventeen restored structures and gardens reflect the unusual life-style of the organization.

Pennsbury Manor, in Bucks County, is the reconstructed plantation of William Penn. The original home was built on land deeded to Penn by the Indians in 1682.

Philadelphia is where the Declaration of Independence and the Constitution of the United States were written and adopted. It was the national capital from 1790 to 1800. Within Independence National Historical Park are the hallmarks of the revolution: Independence Hall, the Liberty Bell, Carpenters' Hall, Old City Hall, Congress Hall, and Franklin Court. Nearby are Elfreth's Alley, the oldest unchanged street in the nation; the Betsy Ross House; Christ Church; and the first, and still the largest, United States Mint.

Pittsburgh's Golden Triangle is located where the Allegheny and Monongahela rivers meet to form the Ohio River. Indians, trappers, settlers, adventurers, and soldiers gathered here. It was the site of Fort Duquesne (French) and Fort Pitt (British) during the French and Indian War. Fort Pitt's original fortifications are part of the Fort Pitt Museum at the site today.

Valley Forge, near King of Prussia, honors General George Washington's poorly equipped Continental army—those who survived the bitter winter of 1777-78, and the three thousand who died there. Within the National Historical Park are the parade ground, the stone house that served as Washington's headquarters, and replicas of the crude huts that sheltered the soldiers.

Wheatland, in Lancaster, was the home of James Buchanan, fifteenth president of the United States. Bought by Buchanan in 1848, it has been restored and refurnished with much of the Buchanans' own furniture, china, and silver.

Other Interesting Places to Visit:

Bethlehem's Eighteenth Century Industrial Area is a grouping of buildings restored and reconstructed to exhibit the industries of the 1760s.

Fallingwater, near Bear Run, was built in 1936 and is an exciting example of the work of architect Frank Lloyd Wright. The house, unique in its dramatic setting and design, is cantilevered over a natural stream and waterfall.

Hershey is the home of the Hershey milk chocolate bar and related products. Street lamps are shaped like Hershey "kisses," the factory visitor center offers a tour of "Chocolate World," and the enticing smell and theme of chocolate is everywhere in this model community planned by founder Milton Hershey in the early 1900s. Hersheypark, originally an amusement park for the chocolate-factory workers, offers rides, shows, a zoo, and a garden.

The Inclined Plane Railway, at Johnstown, built after the devastating flood of 1889, ascends the Allegheny Mountains from the business section of Johnstown to the town of Westmont and offers a grand view of the countryside.

Pennsylvania Dutch Country is the general name for the counties of Lancaster, York, and Berks, where Amish and Mennonite families still live on and work the

Fallingwater, designed by architect Frank Lloyd Wright, was built over a natural stream and waterfall.

land in traditional ways and where visitors may buy their handicrafts and taste their foods. The Farmers Market in downtown Lancaster has been in operation since 1730. Lititz, near the city of Lancaster, contains the nation's oldest pretzel bakery.

Pennsylvania Farm Museum of Landis Valley, near Lancaster, is an outdoor museum that showcases Pennsylvania's rural heritage. Exhibit buildings include a schoolhouse, a general store, and a blacksmith shop. Cooking and craft demonstrations help to interpret the everyday past.

Pine Creek Gorge, near Wellsboro, is called Pennsylvania's Grand Canyon. The gorge follows the Pine Creek River.

The Poconos, the general name for Pennsylvania's northeastern mountain playland, offer resorts, amusement parks, musical and theatrical performances, and seasonal sports. Its scenic beauties include Bushkill, Canoga, and the five-tiered Winona waterfalls; Lake Wallenpaupack; and the Delaware Water Gap.

The State Capitol in Harrisburg is a six-building complex that was built between 1893 and 1906. The main building features floor-to-ceiling murals of Pennsylvania history.

Thomas Bridge, crossing over Crooked Creek in Indiana County, is one of Pennsylvania's more than two hundred remaining covered bridges. Built in 1879, Thomas Bridge is the longest of the fifty covered bridges in the county.

Williamsport, in Lycoming County, was the birthplace of Little League Baseball in 1939. It is international headquarters for all United States and foreign leagues today and the site of the Little League International Museum.

121

IMPORTANT DATES

1500s—Lenape Indians, also known as the Delaware, inhabit much of southeastern Pennsylvania

1600s—Shawnee migrate into Pennsylvania from Kentucky and North Carolina

1614—Dutch explorer Cornelius Mey sails into the lower reaches of the Delaware River

1615—French explorer Etienne Brulé follows the Susquehanna from headwaters to mouth

1616—Dutch explorer Cornelius Hendricksen sails up the Delaware to the mouth of the Schuylkill

1638—New Sweden, first European settlement in Pennsylvania, established near Philadelphia

1643—Johann Printz, governor of "New Sweden," arrives and builds a home, mill, and seat of government at Tinicum Island

1655—Dutch troops from New Netherlands (New York) capture New Sweden

1664—British drive Dutch out of Pennsylvania

1681—Charles II grants 45,000 sq. mi. (116,550 km²) of land, almost all of what is now Pennsylvania, to Admiral Penn, father of William Penn

1682—William Penn arrives on the schooner *Welcome* and draws up plans for colonial government and the city of Philadelphia

1683—First council and assembly meet at Philadelphia and enact Penn's "Charter of Liberties"; Francis Daniel Pastorius founds Germantown

1690—William Rittenhouse establishes the colonies' first paper mill in Wissahickon Valley

1723—Benjamin Franklin arrives in Philadelphia

1729—The *American Weekly Mercury* begins publication in Philadelphia

1731—Franklin founds the first circulation library in the colonies

1732—Samuel Nutt begins to manufacture steel at his Coventry Forge in Chester County; Franklin publishes the first issue of the annual *Poor Richard's Almanack*

1736—Franklin founds the first volunteer fire company in the colonies

1737—"Walking purchase" negotiated between Indians and settlers

1751—Dr. Benjamin Rush founds first hospital in colonies

1759—Building of Fort Pitt completed; bituminous (soft) coal discovered near Pittsburgh

1762—Anthracite (hard) coal discovered in Wyoming Valley

1763—Charles Mason and Jeremiah Dixon begin their four-year survey to set the Mason and Dixon's line boundary between Pennsylvania and Maryland; British troops end Pontiac's War, defeating the Indians at the Battle of Bushy Run

1768—Pennsylvania assembly declares to the British "no taxation without representation"

1774—First Continental Congress opens in Philadelphia

1775—Second Continental Congress opens in Philadelphia and Washington is elected commander-in-chief of the Continental army

1776—Declaration of Independence accepted; Liberty bell rings; Washington crosses the Delaware to defeat the British at Trenton

1777—British occupy Philadelphia; Continental army defeated at Germantown; Washington camps for the winter at Valley Forge

1778—Washington's troops march out of Valley Forge a renewed army; British evacuate Philadelphia; three hundred settlers killed in the Wyoming Massacre

1780—Pennsylvania passes a law declaring that all blacks born in the state are free

1787—Constitutional Convention meets at Philadelphia; Pennsylvania ratifies the Constitution and becomes the second state of the Union on December 12

1792—Purchase of the Erie Triangle completes Pennsylvania's boundaries; United States Mint established at Philadelphia; four thousand die in Philadelphia's yellow-fever epidemic

1794—Whiskey Rebellion

1797—The *United States*, the nation's first frigate, is launched at Philadelphia

1812—State capital established at Harrisburg

1813—Oliver Hazard Perry defeats the British navy in the Battle of Lake Erie

1829—Pennsylvania's first commercial railway begins operation

1859—First commercially successful oil well in the nation is drilled at Titusville

1863—Battle of Gettysburg

1876—John Wanamaker opens the nation's first department store, the Grand Depot, in Philadelphia; the United States Centennial Exposition held in Fairmount Park, Philadelphia

1881—Pittsburgh railroad strike leads to organization of the American Federation of Labor

1889—More than two thousand persons killed in the Johnstown Flood

1901—Philadelphia holds its first annual Mummers' Parade on New Year's Day

1906—Pennsylvania State Capitol is completed

1920—Radio station KDKA in Pittsburgh pioneers commercial broadcasting in the nation

1940—First link of the Pennsylvania Turnpike opens (completed in 1951)

1957—Pennsylvania opens the nation's first full-scale nuclear power plant for civilian use

1968—Pennsylvania adopts a new state constitution

1972—Hurricane Agnes sweeps through eastern Pennsylvania, costing fifty-five lives and $3 billion in property damage

1979—Nation's worst commercial nuclear accident occurs at the Three Mile Island Nuclear Power Plant near Harrisburg

1984—W. Wilson Goode becomes Philadelphia's first black mayor

1985—Philadelphia mayor Goode approves police plan to bomb a radical group sheltered in Philadelphia, resulting in the destruction of one square block in the city and eleven deaths

1987—Pennsylvania hosts *We The People 200,* a year-long celebration of the two-hundredth anniversary of the adoption of the United States Constitution at Philadelphia

1988—The collapse of an oil-storage tank a few miles south of Pittsburgh pours 1 million gallons (3.8 million liters) of diesel oil into the Monongahela and Ohio rivers, creating the biggest inland oil spill in United States history

IMPORTANT PEOPLE

Louisa May Alcott (1832-1888), born in Germantown; novelist; best known for *Little Women* (1868) and *Little Men* (1871), which tell the story of four sisters growing up during and after the Civil War

Richard Allen (1760-1831), born a slave in Philadelphia; clergyman; purchased his own freedom (1796); prominent black leader who was a founder and the first bishop of the African Methodist Episcopal Church

Marian Anderson (1902-   ), born in Philadelphia; operatic and spiritual singer; first black performer at New York City's Metropolitan Opera House (1955); alternate delegate to the United Nations (1958); received one of the first five Kennedy Center Honors (1978)

MARIAN ANDERSON

James (Maxwell) Anderson (1888-1959), born in Atlantic; playwright; received the 1933 Pulitzer Prize in drama for *Both Your Houses*; wrote musicals with Kurt Weill, including *Knickerbocker Holiday* (1938) and *Lost in the Stars* (1949)

Samuel Barber (1910-1981), born in West Chester; composer of operatic and classical music; became first American composer whose work was performed at the Salzburg Festival (*Symphony No. 1*, in 1935); twice received a Pulitzer Prize in music—for the opera *Vanessa* (1958) and for *Piano Concerto* (1963)

SAMUEL BARBER

Ethel Barrymore (1879-1959), born in Philadelphia; actress; noted for her portrayals of Shakespeare's Juliet, Ibsen's Nora, and Miss Moffat in *The Corn is Green* (1940); won an Academy Award for best supporting actress in *None But the Lonely Heart* (1944)

John Barrymore (1882-1942), born in Philadelphia; actor and matinee idol; most famous member of the acting family, noted especially for his stage portrayal of Shakespeare's Hamlet

ETHEL BARRYMORE

John Bartram (1699-1777), born near Darby; botanist, plant collector, and hybridizer; called the "father of American botany"; founded the first botanical garden in the colonies near Philadelphia (1728); named "Botanist to the King" by George II (1765)

Stephen Vincent Benét (1898-1943), born in Bethlehem; poet and novelist; won Pulitzer Prizes in poetry for *John Brown's Body* (1929) and for *Western Star* (1943); also wrote the well-known short story *The Devil and Daniel Webster* (1937)

Nicholas Biddle (1786-1844), born in Philadelphia; author and public official; wrote *The History of the Expedition Under the Command of Captains Lewis and Clark* (1814, from the explorer's records) and edited the nation's first literary magazine, *Portfolio* (1812); Pennsylvania state representative (1810-11); Pennsylvania state senator (1814-17); president of the Bank of the United States (1823-36)

STEPHEN VINCENT BENÉT

125

ALEXANDER CALDER

ANDREW CARNEGIE

RACHEL CARSON

WILT CHAMBERLAIN

Anthony Joseph Bevilacqua (1923-   ); in 1987 succeeded seventy-seven-year-old Cardinal John Joseph Krol as Archbishop of Philadelphia

James Buchanan (1791-1868), born in Cove Gap, near Mercersburg; fifteenth president of the United States, whose presidency saw the beginning of the secession crisis that led to the Civil War; U.S. representative (1821-31); U.S. senator (1834-45); secretary of state under President Polk; minister to Russia (1832-34); ambassador to Great Britain (1853-56); president (1857-61)

Alexander Calder (1898-1976), born in Philadelphia; sculptor; best known for creating mobiles or moving sculptures of aluminum, brass, or steel wired together and given motion by air currents

Andrew Carnegie (1835-1919); steel-industry pioneer and philanthropist; founder and president of Carnegie Steel Company (now USX Corporation); introduced the Bessemer (open-furnace) steel-making process to the nation; donated more than $350 million, establishing more than 2,500 libraries, the Carnegie Institute of Pittsburgh, the Carnegie Institution at Washington, and the Carnegie Corporation at New York

Rachel Carson (1907-1964), born in Springdale; marine biologist and author; her best-known book, *Silent Spring* (1962), aroused public awareness of the dangers of pesticide poisoning and led to the banning of the pesticide DDT

Mary Cassatt (1847-1926), born in Allegheny City; Impressionist artist; best known for her works on the theme of mother and child; her paintings *The Boating Party* (1883) and *Morning Toilette* (1886) are exhibited at the National Gallery in Washington, D.C.

Wilton (Wilt) Chamberlain (1936-   ), born in Philadelphia; professional basketball player; in his fourteen-year career was named Rookie of the Year (1959-60) and Most Valuable Player four times, led the NBA in scoring for a record seven straight years, and scored a record 100 points in one game (1962)

(Avram) Noam Chomsky (1928-   ), born in Philadelphia; linguist and educator, developed the theory of transformational grammar, a system for describing the rules that determine any possible sentence in any language

Roberto Clemente (1934-1972); professional baseball player; in his eighteen-season career with the Pittsburgh Pirates won four National League batting titles; voted the league's Most Valuable Player (1966); selected to the All-Star team twelve times; elected to the Baseball Hall of Fame after his death in an airplane crash while working for the relief of Nicaraguan earthquake victims

George Mifflin Dallas (1792-1864), born in Philadelphia; public official; vice-president of the United States (1845-49); U.S. senator (1831-33); attorney general of Pennsylvania (1833); U.S. minister to Russia (1837-39) and Great Britain (1856-61)

John Dickinson (1732-1808); lawyer and revolutionary war patriot; Pennsylvania legislator (1762); member of the Continental Congress (1774-76) and the Constitutional Convention (1787); wrote the first draft of the Articles of Confederation (1776); founder of Dickinson College at Carlisle

W. C. Fields (1880-1946), born William Claude Dukenfield in Philadelphia; motion-picture, stage, and radio comedian; best remembered for creating the film character who hated dogs, children, policemen, bankers, and wives in such films as *You Can't Cheat an Honest Man* (1939), *The Bank Dick* (1940), *My Little Chickadee* (1940, with Mae West), and *Never Give a Sucker an Even Break* (1941)

W.C. FIELDS

John Fitch (1743-1798); inventor; built the first practical steamboat; began the world's first regularly scheduled steamboat service (1790), between Philadelphia and Burlington, New Jersey

Stephen Collins Foster (1826-1864), born in Lawrenceville (now part of Pittsburgh); composer; wrote more than two hundred popular songs, including "Old Folks at Home" (1851), "My Old Kentucky Home" (1853), and "Jeanie with the Light Brown Hair" (1854)

Benjamin Franklin (1706-1790); revolutionary war patriot, statesman, diplomat, inventor, and author; settled in Philadelphia at the age of seventeen and founded there the nation's first public library and the city's first fire company; helped write the Declaration of Independence and the U.S. Constitution; held numerous positions in colonial, state, and national government

BENJAMIN FRANKLIN

Henry Clay Frick (1849-1919), born in West Overton; industrialist and philanthropist; established the H.C. Frick Coke Company and became a millionaire by the age of thirty; willed a large part of his fortune to hospitals, schools, and a park in Pittsburgh, and to establish New York City's Frick Art Museum

Robert Fulton (1765-1815), born in Lancaster County; inventor, artist, and engineer; built the first commercially successful steamboat (launched 1807); developed a submarine for the French government, and the first steam-powered warship for the U.S. government

HENRY CLAY FRICK

Stephen Girard (1750-1831); businessman, banker, and philanthropist; helped set up the Second Bank of the United States (1816); bequeathed most of his $7 million fortune to found Girard College in Philadelphia (opened 1848) and to municipal improvements, including the police system in Philadelphia

Martha Graham (1894-1991), born in Pittsburgh; dancer, choreographer; helped develop and popularize modern dance, created dance-dramas using such uniquely American themes as the New England heritage, in *Appalachian Spring* (1944), and southwestern culture, in *El Penitente* (1940)

MARTHA GRAHAM

WINFIELD S. HANCOCK

GEORGE S. KAUFMAN

GRACE KELLY

CONNIE MACK

Alexander Meigs Haig, Jr. (1924-   ), born in Philadelphia; career army officer and public official; four-star general; White House chief of staff (1973); supreme commander of NATO (North Atlantic Treaty Organization) forces in Europe (1974-75); U.S. secretary of state (1981-82)

Winfield Scott Hancock (1824-1886), born in Montgomery Square; career army officer and political leader; Union general in the Civil War; played a pivotal role at Gettysburg; district commander in the South during Reconstruction

Henry John Heinz (1844-1919), born in Pittsburgh; a founder of F. & J. Heinz, the prepared-foods company that uses the "57 Varieties" slogan

Louis Isadore Kahn (1902-1974); architect; professor at Yale University (1947-57) and the University of Pennsylvania (1957-74); one of the buildings he designed is the Yale University Art Gallery

George Simon Kaufman (1889-1961), born in Pittsburgh; playwright and director; drama critic of the *New York Times* (1917-30); best known for collaborations with Edna Ferber on *Dinner at Eight* (1932) and *Stage Door* (1936), and with Moss Hart on the Pulitzer Prizewinning *You Can't Take It With You* (1936) and *The Man Who Came to Dinner* (1939)

Eugene Curran (Gene) Kelly (1912-   ), born in Pittsburgh; dancer, singer, actor, and director; noted for athletic dance sequences combining tap and ballet in such musical films as *An American in Paris* (1951) and *Singin' in the Rain* (1952); received the American Film Institute's Lifetime Achievement Award in 1985

Grace Patrick Kelly (1929-1982), born in Philadelphia; actress, Princess of Monaco; won 1954 Academy Award for best actress in the film *The Country Girl*; married Prince Rainier III of Monaco (1956)

Philander Chase Knox (1853-1921), born in Brownsville; lawyer and public official; U.S. attorney general (1901-04); senator (1904-09 and 1917-21); secretary of state (1909-13)

Connie Mack (1862-1956), born Cornelius McGillicuddy; Hall of Fame baseball manager; helped organize the American League; owner-manager of the Philadelphia Athletics (1901-50), led team into nine World Series

George Brinton McClellan (1826-1885), born in Philadelphia; career army officer and political leader; Union general during the Civil War; governor of New Jersey (1878-81)

William Holmes McGuffey (1800-1873), born in Washington County; educator; best known for compiling the six *McGuffey's Readers* (1836-57), which sold more than 120 million copies and were widely used in schools to promote a moral education

George Catlett Marshall (1880-1959), born in Uniontown; career army officer and diplomat; chief of staff of the U.S. Army during World War II; became the only person ever to serve as both secretary of state (1947-49) and secretary of defense (1950-51); formulated the United States' strong anti-Soviet policy, which included the Truman Doctrine of aid to non-Communist nations and the Marshall Plan of economic reconstruction for war-torn Western Europe; received the Nobel Peace Prize in 1953

GEORGE C. MARSHALL

Margaret Mead (1901-1978), born in Philadelphia; pioneer anthropologist whose South Pacific fieldwork resulted in the texts *Coming of Age in Samoa* (1928) and *Sex and Temperament in Three Primitive Societies* (1935); championed the use of anthropological films to record and study primitive cultures

George Gordon Meade (1815-1872); army officer; best remembered for his leadership in the Civil War; brigadier general (1863); repulsed Confederate army under General Robert E. Lee at Battle of Gettysburg (1863)

MARGARET MEAD

Andrew William Mellon (1855-1937), born in Pittsburgh; financier, public official, and philanthropist; U.S. secretary of the treasury (1921-32); founded the town of Donora, where he built a large steel plant; established the Mellon Institute in Pittsburgh and the National Gallery of Art in Washington, D.C.

Robert Morris (1734-1806); financier and revolutionary war patriot; member of the Continental Congress (1775-78), signer of the Declaration of Independence; delegate to the Constitutional Convention (1787); as U.S. superintendent of finance (1781-84), worked to establish a national mint and a national bank; U.S. senator (1789-95)

LUCRETIA MOTT

Lucretia Coffin Mott (1793-1880); Quaker minister and social reformer; settled in Philadelphia in 1809; helped found the American Anti-Slavery Society and the Philadelphia Anti-Slavery Society, the Seneca Falls (Women's Rights) Convention, and the American Equal Rights Association

Joseph William (Joe) Namath (1943-   ), born in Beaver Falls; Hall of Fame football player and actor

Clifford Odets (1906-1963), born in Philadelphia; dramatist and film scriptwriter; best known for social protest themes in such plays as *Waiting for Lefty* (1935), about a taxi-drivers' strike

THOMAS PAINE

John Henry O'Hara (1905-1970), born in Pottsville; novelist; used the imaginary Gibbsville, Pennsylvania as the setting for many of his novels; best known for *Butterfield 8* (1935), *A Rage To Live* (1949), *From the Terrace* (1958), and *Pal Joey* (1940)

Thomas Paine (1737-1809); author and revolutionary war patriot; lived in Philadelphia (1774-87) during the revolutionary war; rallied the colonists to the cause of independence with the popular and influential pamphlet *Common Sense* (1776)

ROBERT PEARY

WILLIAM PENN

GIFFORD PINCHOT

BENJAMIN RUSH

Charles Willson Peale (1741-1827); artist and amateur natural scientist; noted for his portraits of famous revolutionary war heroes; opened the nation's first museum of natural history objects, Indian artifacts, and portraits at Philadelphia's Independence Hall in 1802; helped organize the first U.S. public art exhibition (1794, in Philadelphia); and helped establish the Pennsylvania Academy of Fine Arts (1805)

Robert Edwin Peary (1856-1920), born in Cresson; Arctic explorer; generally credited as the first person to reach the North Pole and document the trip

William Penn (1644-1718); founder of Pennsylvania; Quaker convert who wanted to establish an ideal colony by guaranteeing settlers religious freedom, an elective assembly and council, and the traditional English liberties; helped plan Philadelphia, summoned the assembly, and established peaceful relations with the Indians

Boies Penrose (1860-1921), born in Philadelphia; political leader; state representative (1884-86), state senator (1887-97), U.S. senator (1897-1921); long-time political boss of Pennsylvania's Republican party and a leading spokesman for the conservative viewpoint in national politics

Gifford Pinchot (1865-1946); public official, forestry expert, and conservationist; founded the National Conservation Association; influenced President Theodore Roosevelt to develop and expand the nation's forest reserves; chief of the Department of Agriculture's Divison of Forestry (now the U.S. Forest Service) (1898-1910); governor of Pennsylvania (1923-27 and 1931-35); founder of and professor at Yale University's Pinchot School of Forestry (1903-36)

Joseph Priestly (1733-1804); scientist and founder of English Unitarianism; discovered several gases, including oxygen; noted for experiments in electricity and plant respiration; settled in Northumberland in 1794

David Rittenhouse (1732-1796), born in Paper Mill Run, near Germantown; astronomer and mathematician; built what may have been the first American-made telescope; Pennsylvania state treasurer (1777-89), first director of the U.S. Mint (1792-95)

Elizabeth (Betsy) Ross (1752-1836), born in Philadelphia; legendary seamstress popularly credited with making the first American flag at the request of George Washington; records do show that she supplied flags to the Pennsylvania navy in 1777

Benjamin Rush (1746-1813), born in Philadelphia; physician and political and social reformer; signer of the Declaration of Independence; pioneer in military hygiene and the treatment of mental illness; promoted improved education for women, the abolition of slavery, and an end to capital punishment; also served as treasurer of the U.S. Mint (1797-1813)

Michael (Mike) Schmidt (1949-   ); professional baseball player; joined the Philadelphia Phillies in 1972; voted Most Valuable Player in National League in 1980, 1981, and 1986; led league in home runs for eight seasons (a league record)

Burrhus Frederic (B.F.) Skinner (1904-1990), born in Susquehanna; psychologist; best known for studies in the learning process and for creating the Baby Box, or Skinner Box, a controlled environment for infants

B.F. SKINNER

Gertrude Stein (1874-1946), born in Allegheny; author; developed a new writing style with minimal punctuation and simple, basic words, often repeated, as in her famous: "Rose is a rose is a rose is a rose"; best known for her *Autobiography of Alice B. Toklas* (1933)

Thaddeus Stevens (1792-1868); political leader and antislavery spokesman in Congress; led the drive to pass Pennsylvania's free public school law as member of the state legislature (1833-41); promoted harsh Reconstruction policies in the South as a U.S. representative (1849-53 and 1859-68)

THADDEUS STEVENS

Thomas Sully (1783-1872); portrait painter; settled in Philadelphia in 1808; best known for *Washington at the Passage of the Delaware* (1819) and his portraits of Thomas Jefferson and General Lafayette

Ida Minerva Tarbell (1857-1944), born in Erie County; author; noted for carefully documented attacks on political and corporate corruption; her *History of the Standard Oil Company* (1904) resulted in federal government action against Standard Oil

Frederick Winslow Taylor (1856-1915), born in Germantown; engineer and efficiency expert; developed time-and-motion study, a system of timing work movements to determine ways of ensuring maximum possible job efficiency

IDA TARBELL

John Updike (1932-   ), born in Shillington; author; noted novelist, poet, book reviewer; received the 1982 Pulitzer Prize in fiction for *Rabbit is Rich*

Anthony Wayne (1745-1796), born near Paoli in Chester County; revolutionary war hero and career soldier; popularly known as "Mad Anthony" for his daredevil exploits; best known for his brilliant victory over the British at Stony Point (1779)

Benjamin West (1738-1820), born in Springfield; artist; painted historic scenes and portraits; became first American artist to win international recognition; his London studio attracted and influenced many students from America; best known for *Penn's Treaty with the Indians* (1772) and *Death on a Pale Horse* (1802)

ANTHONY WAYNE

George Westinghouse (1846-1914); inventor and manufacturer; original Westinghouse Electric and Manufacturing Company was formed in 1886 in a small factory in Pittsburgh; through inventions, technological innovations, and manufacture of electrical machinery contributed to the development of the electrical age

ANDREW WYETH

David Wilmot (1814-1868), born in Bethany; political leader; sponsored the Wilmot Proviso (1854) to ban slavery in new territory acquired from Mexico; U.S. representative (1845-51) and U.S. senator (1861); helped found the Republican party (1854)

James Wilson (1742-1798); patriot and lawyer; signer of the Declaration of Independence; member of the Continental Congress (1774, 1775-77, 1782-83, and 1785-86); helped draft the U.S. Constitution and the Pennsylvania state constitution; associate justice of the U.S. Supreme Court (1789-98)

Andrew Wyeth (1917-   ), born in Chadds Ford; artist; best known for his realistic portraits and scenes in nature, especially *Tenant Farmer* (1961) and *Christina's World* (1948)

Newell Convers (N.C.) Wyeth (1882-1945); painter and illustrator; father of Andrew Wyeth; one of America's foremost illustrators; lived and painted in the Brandywine Valley

GOVERNORS

Benjamin Franklin	1785-1788	Samuel W. Pennypacker	1903-1907
Thomas Mifflin	1788-1799	Edwin Sydney Stuart	1907-1911
Thomas McKean	1799-1808	John Kinley Tener	1911-1915
Simon Snyder	1808-1817	Martin Grove Brumbaugh	1915-1919
William Findlay	1817-1820	William Cameron Sproul	1919-1923
Joseph Hiester	1820-1823	Gifford Pinchot	1923-1927
John Andrew Shulze	1823-1829	John Stuchell Fisher	1927-1931
George Wolf	1829-1835	Gifford Pinchot	1931-1935
Joseph Ritner	1835-1839	George Howard Earle	1935-1939
David Rittenhouse Porter	1839-1845	Arthur Horace James	1939-1943
Francis Rawn Shunk	1845-1848	Edward Martin	1943-1947
William Freame Johnston	1848-1852	John C. Bell, Jr.	1947
William Bigler	1852-1855	James H. Duff	1947-1951
James Pollock	1855-1858	John S. Fine	1951-1955
William Fisher Packer	1858-1861	George Michael Leader	1955-1959
Andrew Gregg Curtin	1861-1867	David Leo Lawrence	1959-1963
John White Geary	1867-1873	William W. Scranton	1963-1967
John Frederick Hartranft	1873-1879	Raymond P. Shafer	1967-1971
Henry Martyn Hoyt	1879-1883	Milton J. Shapp	1971-1979
Robert Emory Pattison	1883-1887	Richard Thornburgh	1979-1987
James Addams Beaver	1887-1891	Robert Casey	1987-
Robert Emory Pattison	1891-1895		
Daniel Hartman Hastings	1895-1899		
William Alexis Stone	1899-1903		

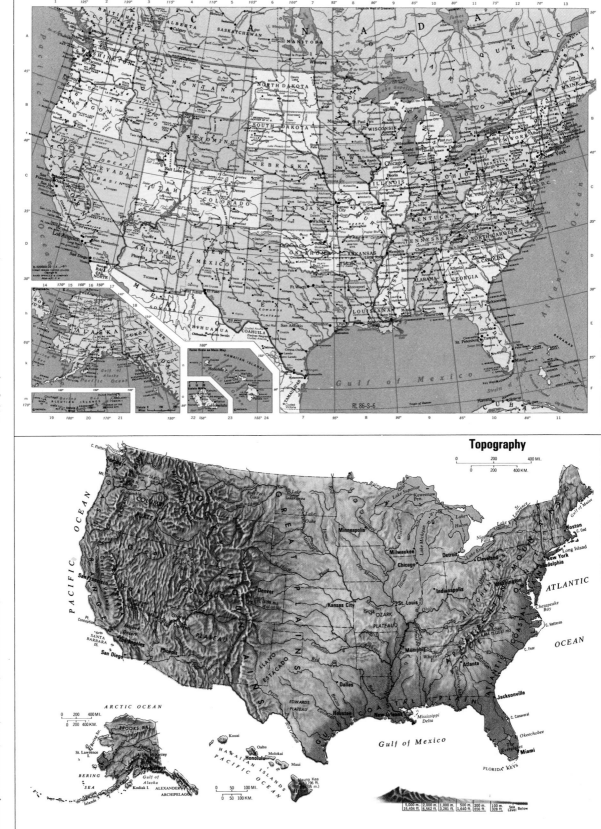

Topography

MAP KEY

Akron	F9
Aliquippa	E1;h13
Allegheny (river)	C2,3,5,6;D,E,F,2,3;h,k14,15
Allegheny Mountains (mountains)	G3,4;F4;E5,6;D6
Allegheny Plateau	E1,2,3,4;D2,3,4,5,6,7;C5,6,7,8
Allentown	E11
Altoona	F5
Ambler	F11;o21
Ambridge	E1;h13
Annville	F8,9
Appalachian Mountains (mountains)	G4,5;F4,5,6,7;E6,7;D7,8,9,10;C10,11
Archbald	m18
Arnold	h14
Ashland	E9
Ashley	n17
Aspinwall	k14
Athens	C9
Avalon	h,k13
Avoca	m18
Babb Creek (creek)	C7
Baden	E1;h13
Baldwin	k14
Bangor	E11
Barnesboro	E4
Beaver	F6,7
Beaver Falls	E1
Beaver Run Reservoir (reservoir)	F2
Bedford	F4
Bellefonte	E6
Belleville	F1;h,k13
Bellevue	F4
Berwick	F6,7
Berwyn	o20
Bethel Park	k14
Bethlehem	E11
Big Knob (mountain)	F6,7
Big Shiney Mountain (mountain)	n18
Birch Rock Hill (mountain)	F3
Birdsboro	F10
Blairsville	F3
Blakely	m18
Bloomsburg	E9
Blue Knob (mountain)	F4
Blue Knob Mountains (mountains)	F6,7
Bowman Creek (creek)	m16,17
Boyertown	h15
Brackenridge	k14
Braddock	C4
Bradford	C1
Brentwood	k14
Bridgeport	o20
Bridgeville	k13
Bristol	F11;o21
Brookville	D3
Brownsville	E2
Butler	E2
California	F2
Camp Hill	F8
Canonsburg	E1
Carbondale	E11
Carlisle	D5
Carmer Hill (hill)	C10,11
Carnegie	k14
Catasauqua	E11
Centerville	F2

Chadds Ford	G10
Chambersburg	G6
Charleroi	F2
Chester	G11;p20
Clairton	F2
Clarion	D3
Clarion (river)	D3
Clarks Summit	m18
Clearfield	D5
Coaldale	E10
Coatesville	F10
Collegeville	F11
Collingdale	p20
Columbia	F9
Conemaugh River Lake (reservoir)	F4
Conemaugh Lake (lake)	F3
Connellsville	F2
Conneaut Lake	F1
Conshohocken	F11;o20
Conway	E1
Coopersburg	E10,11
Coplay	E11
Coraopolis	h13
Cornwall	F9
Coudersport	C5
Crafton	k13
Crooked (creek)	E4
Crooked Creek Lake	E3
Curwensville	E4
Curwensville Lake (lake)	E4
Dallas	D10;m17
Dallastown	G8
Danville	E8
Darby	G11
Delaware (river)	D,E,F,G10,11,12;p20,21;o21,22
Delaware Water Gap	D11;o18
Derry	F3
Dickson City	D10;m18
Donora	F2
Dormont	k13
Downingtown	F,G10
Doylestown	F11
Drifton	E10
Dunmore	D10;m18
Dupont	n17,18
Duquesne	F2;k14
Duryea	D10;m17
East Branch Clarion River Lake (reservoir)	D4
East Butler	E2
East Petersburg	F9
East Stroudsburg	E11
Easton	E11
Economy	k14
Ebensburg	F4
Edinboro	D8,9
Edwardsville	o19
Elizabethtown	F9
Ellwood City	C7
Emmaus	F8
Emporium	G2
Emsworth	E9,10
Ephrata	F1;k13
Erie	F2;k14
Etna	D10;n17
Exeter	D1
Farrell	F2

Fayetteville	G6
First Fork (Fork River)	F2
Fisher	F10
Fleetwood	E2
Ford City	D10;n17
Forest Hills	E9
Forty Fort	D2
Fountain Hill	D2
Frackville	D10
Franklin	B,C,2
Freeland	F4
French Creek (Creek)	D5
Gelstown	G7
George B. Stevenson Reservoir (flood-control reservoir)	F10
Gettysburg	p20
Gilbertsville	G6
Glassport	F2
Glenolden	D1
Greencastle	E10
Greensburg	D11
Greenville	G8
Grove City	D11
Hamburg	m16
Hamlin	m16
Hanover	E10
Hardwood Ridge (ridge)	E11
Harrisburg	F8
Harveys Lake (lake)	F8
Harveys Creek (creek)	F5
Hazelton	k14
Hellertown	C1
Hershey	F5,6
Highspire	p13
Hollidaysburg	E3
Homestead	p20
Honesdale	k13
Hopewell	F4
Huntingdon	G10
Imperial	C5
Independence National Historical Park	k13
Indiana	F9
Ingram	C2
Irwin	C5
Jacks Mountain (mountains)	k13
Jeannette	E4
Jenkintown	E3,h?
Jersey Shore	F2
Jessup	E10,11
Jim Thorpe	G8
Johnsonburg	E4
Johnstown	D10;m17
Juniata (river)	G8
Kane	E8
Kennett Square	G11
Kettle Creek (creek)	F9
Kettle Creek Lake (lake)	D10;m18
Kingston	n17,18
Kulpmont	F2;k14
Kutztown	D10;m17
Lake Arthur (lake)	D4
Lake Erie (lake)	E2
Lake Wallenpaupack (lake)	F9
Lancaster	E11
Lansdale	E11
Lansford	k14
Larksville	D8,9
Latrobe	o19
Laureldale	F9
Lawrence	C7
Lawrence Park	F8
Lebanon	G2
Leechburg	E9,10
Lehigh (River)	F1;k13
Lehighton	F2;k14
Lemoyne	D10;n17
Levittown	D1

Lewisburg	E8
Lewistown	F7
Liberty	C7
Lititz	F9
Littlestown	G7
Lock Haven	D7
Loyalsock Creek (creek)	D8,9
Lyzoming Creek (creek)	D7
Lyndora	E2
Malvern	o20
Manheim	F9
Mansfield	C8
Marietta	F9
Masontown	G2
McAdoo	E10
McKees Rocks	k13
McKeesport	F2;k14
Meadville	C1
Mechanicsburg	F8

Media	G11;p20
Middletown	F8
Midland	E1
Mifflinburg	E7
Millersburg	E8
Millersville	F9
Milton	E8
Minersville	E9
Monaca	E1
Monessen	F2
Monongahela	F2
Monongahela (river)	F,G2
Monroeville	k14
Montoursville	D8
Moosic	m18
Moosic Mountains (mountains)	m,n18
Mount Carmel	E9
Mount Davis (mountain)	G3
Mount Joy	F9
Mount Lebanon	k13
Mount Penn	F10
Mount Pleasant	F2
Mount Union	F6
Muncy	D8
Munhall	k14
Myerstown	F9
Nanticoke	n17
Nanty Glo	F4
Narberth	o20
Nazareth	E11
Nesquehoning	E10
New Brighton	E1
New Castle	D1
New Cumberland	F8
New Holland	F9
New Kensington	E1
New Wilmington	D1
Norristown	F11;o20
North East	C2
North Wales	F11
Northampton	E11
Northumberland	E8
Norwood	p20
Oakmont	E,F2;h,k14
Octoraro Creek (creek)	G9,10
Ohio (river)	D7
Ohioville	D7
Oil City	C,D2
Oil (creek)	C2
Old Forge	D10;m18
Oliver	G2
Olyphant	D10;m18
Orwigsburg	E9
Oxford	G10
Palmerton	E10
Palmyra	F8,o,p21
Paoli	o20
Pen Argyl	E11
Penbrook	F8
Perkasie	F11
Philadelphia	G11;p21
Philadelphia Naval Shipyard	p21
Phillipsburg	E5
Phoenixville	F10;o19
Pikes Rocks (mountain)	C3
Pine Creek (creek)	C6,7
Pine Creek Gorge (gorge)	C6,7
Pitcairn	k14
Pittsburgh	F2;k14
Pittston	n17
Plains	n17
Plum	k14
Plumsteadville	F11
Plymouth	D10;n17
Pocono Mountains (mountains)	D,E,10,11
Portage	F4
Pottstown	F10
Pottsville	E9
Prospect Park	p20
Punxsutawney	E4
Pymatuning Reservoir (reservoir)	C,D1
Quakertown	F11
Rankin	k14
Raystown Branch (river)	F5
Reading	F10
Red Lion	G8
Reynoldsville	D4
Ridgway	D4
Ridley Park	p20
Rixford	C4
Roaring Spring	F5
Rochester	E1
Royersford	F10
Saint Clair	E9
Saint Marys	D4
Sayre	C9
Schuylkill (river)	F10;o20,21;p21

Schuylkill Haven	E9
Scottdale	F2
Scranton	D10;m18
Selinsgrove	E8
Sellersville	F11
Sewickley	E8
Shamokin	E9
Sharon	D1
Sharon Hill	p20
Sharpsburg	k14
Sharpsville	D1
Shenandoah	E9
Shillington	F10
Shippensburg	F6,7
Sinnemahoning Creek (creek)	C,D5,6
Slatington	E10
Slippery Rock	D1
Somerset	F3
Souderton	F11
South Williamsport	D7
Spring Brook (brook)	m,n18
Spring City	F10
Springdale	k14
Springfield	p20
State College	E6
Steelton	F8
Stowe	F10
Stroudsburg	E11
Sugar Creek (creek)	D2
Sugar Creek (creek)	C8,9
Summit Hill	E10
Sunbury	E8
Susquehanna	C10
Susquehanna (river)	C8,9,D8,9,10,E8,F7,8,G9,10;n17
Susquehanna, West Branch (river)	D,E,4,5,6,7
Swissvale	k14
Swoyerville	n17
Tamaqua	E10
Tarentum	E2;h14
Taylor	D10;m18
Telford	F11
Throop	m18
Tioga (river)	C7
Tionesta Creek (creek)	C,D3
Tionesta Lake (lake)	D3
Titusville	C2
Towanda	C9
Towanda Creek (creek)	C8,9
Trafford	k14
Turtle Creek	F,G5,6
Tuscarora (mountains)	E5
Tyrone	G2
Union City	C2
Uniontown	G2
Upper Darby	G11;p20
Valley Forge	o20
Vandergrift	E2
Vanport	F1;h14
Verona	E2
Warminster	h,k14
Warren	C3
Washington	F1
Waynesboro	G6
Waynesburg	G1
Weatherly	E10
Wellersburg	G4
Wellsboro	C7
Wesleyville	B2
West Chester	G10
West Hazleton	E10
West Mifflin	k14
West Newton	F2
West Norriton	o20
West Pittston	D10,11
West Reading	F10
West View	h13
West Wyoming	m,n17
West York	G8
Westmont	F4
Wheatland	D1
Wilkes-Barre	D10;n17
Wilkinsburg	F2;k14
Williamsport	D7
Willow Grove Naval Air Station	F11
Wilson	E11
Windber	F4
Windgap	F2
Wyoming	C4
Wyomissing	F10
Yeadon	p20
York	G8
Youghiogheny (river)	F,G2,3
Youghiogheny River Lake (reservoir)	G2,3
Youngwood	F2
Zelienope	E1

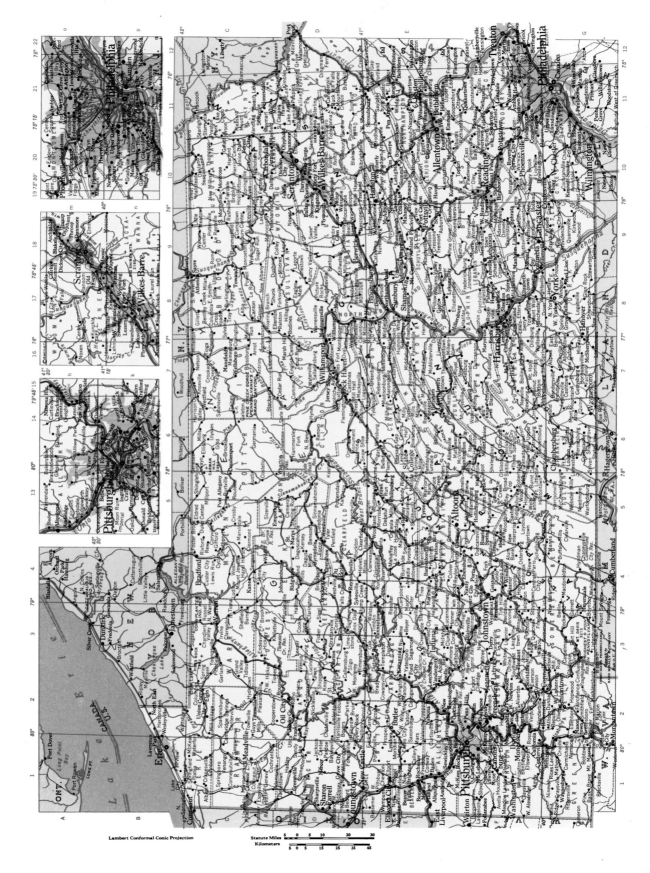

Lambert Conformal Conic Projection

Statute Miles
Kilometers

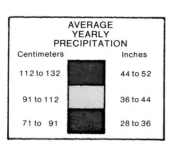

AVERAGE YEARLY PRECIPITATION

Centimeters		Inches
112 to 132		44 to 52
91 to 112		36 to 44
71 to 91		28 to 36

MAJOR HIGHWAYS

NATURAL GAS
OIL
MINING
MANUFACTURING
NURSERY PRODUCTS
MAPLE SYRUP
DAIRY PRODUCTS
BEEF CATTLE
HOGS
SHEEP
POULTRY

TOBACCO
BUCKWHEAT
WHEAT
CORN
OATS
SOYBEANS
POTATOES
VEGETABLES
FRUIT
GRAPES

POPULATION DENSITY

Number of persons per square kilometer		Number of persons per square mile
More than 200		More than 500
100 to 200		250 to 500
20 to 100		50 to 250
Less than 20		Less than 50

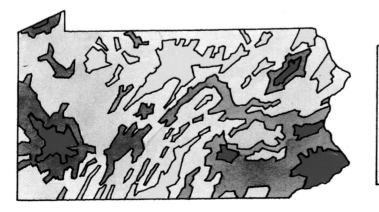

TOPOGRAPHY

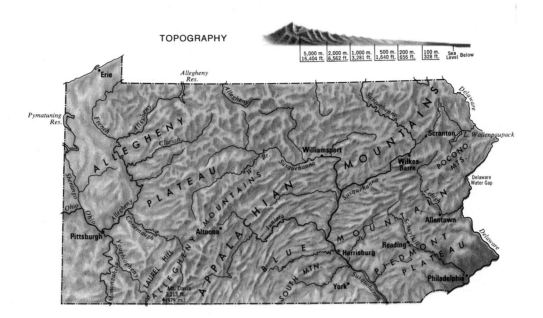

5,000 m.	2,000 m.	1,000 m.	500 m.	200 m.	100 m.	Sea	Below
16,404 ft.	6,562 ft.	3,281 ft.	1,640 ft.	656 ft.	328 ft.	Level	

Courtesy of Hammond, Incorporated

Maplewood, New Jersey

COUNTIES

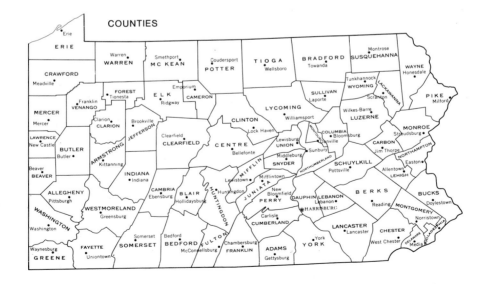

This
Lancaster
County
farm
shimmers
in a
dawn mist.

INDEX

Page numbers that appear in boldface type indicate illustrations.

A traditional
Pennsylvania
house in winter

Picture Identifications

Front cover: Pittsburgh's Golden Triangle
Back cover: Amish buggy on a Lancaster County road
Pages 2-3: Scenic view of the setting of French Azilum from an overlook across the Susquehanna River between Wysox and Wyalusing
Page 6: Independence Hall, Philadelphia
Pages 8-9: Autumn view of a valley from Hawk Mountain
Pages 16-17: Montage of Pennsylvanians
Page 22: *The Landing of William Penn, 1682*, an oil painting by J.L.G. Ferris
Pages 32-33: *The Declaration of Independence, July 4, 1776*, an oil painting by John Trumbull
Pages 44-45: A wagon train on the road during the era of westward expansion
Page 56: Chutes loading coal onto canal boats on the Lehigh Canal
Page 66: The Capitol, Harrisburg
Pages 76-77: Night view of Three Rivers Stadium, Pittsburgh
Page 76 (inset): Logan Circle, Philadelphia
Pages 90-91: Night view of Pittsburgh
Page 91 (inset): Independence Hall, Philadelphia
Page 108: Montage showing the state flag, the state bird (ruffed grouse), the state tree (Eastern hemlock), the state flower (mountain laurel), and the state animal (white-tailed deer)

About the Author

Deborah Kent grew up in Little Falls, New Jersey. She received a Bachelor of Arts degree in English from Oberlin College, a Master's Degree from the Smith College School for Social Work, and a Master of Fine Arts degree from the University of Guanajuato in Mexico. Ms. Kent worked in a New York City settlement house and taught disabled children in Mexico before she began to write full-time. For two years she lived in the central Pennsylvania town of Lewisburg, and spent many weekends exploring the highways and back roads of the Keystone State.

Deborah Kent is the author of several novels for young adults as well as other books in the *America the Beautiful* series. She lives in Chicago with her husband and their daughter Janna.

Picture Acknowledgments

H. Armstrong Roberts: © H. Abernathy: Front cover; © J. Irwin: Back cover; © Ralph Krubner: Page 101 (left)
© **SuperStock International:** Pages 2-3, 5, 6, 40, 90-91, 107 (bottom right)
Nawrocki Stock Photo: © Jeff Apoian: Pages 4, 8-9, 13 (left), 87 (inset), 107 (top left), 111; © Mike J. Howell: Page 17 (bottom right); © Jim Polaski: Page 64; © Rui Coutinho: Page 91 (inset); © Frank J. Neiman: Page 96 (top right)
Root Resources: © James Blank: Page 11; © Joseph Nettis: Pages 16 (top left), 17 (bottom left), 38, 63 (right), 88 (top right and bottom), 107 (top right and bottom left), 118; © MacDonald: Pages 63 (left), 96 (center right); © Kitty Kohout: Page 108 (tree); © Alan G. Nelson: Page 108 (bottom right)
© **Mary Ann Brockman:** Pages 12, 16 (center right and bottom right), 25, 66, 69 (all photos), 70 (both photos), 71 (right), 75 (top left), 76 (inset), 95, 96 (top left, bottom left, bottom right), 98 (both photos), 102, 105
Reinhard Brucker: Page 13 (center, inset)
Photri: Pages 16 (top right), 17 (top left), 31, 76-77, 83, 104, 127 (bottom), 129 (Mead); © Leonard Lee Rue: Pages 13 (right), 108 (bottom left); © D. Long: Page 16 (center left); © Spillane: Page 16 (bottom left); © M. Long: Page 21; © Eugene L. Drifmeyer: Page 75 (right); © Ken Kaminsky: Page 88 (left); © Tracy Wetherby: Page 121
Marilyn Gartman Agency: © Michael Philip Manheim: Pages 17 (top right), 84 (top left and bottom); © G.A. Reims: Pages 101 (right), 141
© **J.L.G. Ferris, Archives of 76, Bay Village, Ohio:** Pages 22, 36
Historical Pictures Service, Inc., Chicago: Pages 26 (both photos), 27, 43, 44-45, 47 (both photos), 48, 49, 52, 55 (both photos), 56, 58, 59 (bottom), 126 (Carnegie and Carson), 127 (Fields and Frick), 128 (top and bottom), 129 (Mott and Paine), 130 (Penn, Pinchot, and Rush), 131 (Skinner, Stevens, and Wayne)
Courtesy of the Pennsylvania Academy of the Fine Arts: Page 28
Yale University Art Gallery: Pages 32-33
Cameramann International Ltd.: Pages 37, 75 (center and bottom left), 93 (both photos), 94
Valley Forge Historical Society: Page 39
Architect of the Capitol: Page 42
Courtesy Sagamore Hill National Historic Site: Page 59 (top left)
The Bettmann Archive: Page 59 (top right)
Wide World Photos: Pages 61, 80 (all photos), 125 (all photos), 126 (top and bottom), 128 (Kaufman and Kelly), 129 (top), 130 (top), 132
R/C Photo Agency: Page 99 (both photos); © Don Larson: Page 71
Roloc Color Slides: Page 72
Drake Well Museum: Page 79 (both photos), 131 (Tarbell)
New York Historical Society: Page 81 (left)
National Gallery of Art: Pages 81 (right), 82
© **Virginia Grimes:** Page 84 (top right)
Courtesy of the Philadelphia Orchestra: Page 87 (left)
Pennsylvania Bureau of Travel Development: Page 100
© **Lynn M. Stone:** Page 108 (top right)
Journalism Services: © Tim McCabe: Page 112
Library of Congress: Page 127 (Franklin)
© **Joseph A. DiChello, Jr.:** Page 138
Len W. Meents: Maps on pages 94, 96, 99, 104, 105, 136
Courtesy Flag Research Center, Winchester, Massachusetts 01890: Flag on page 108